Handbook for
FRENCH COMPOSITION

PRENTICE-HALL INTERNATIONAL, INC., *London*
PRENTICE-HALL OF AUSTRALIA, PTY., LTD., *Sydney*
PRENTICE-HALL OF CANADA, LTD., *Toronto*
PRENTICE-HALL OF INDIA (PRIVATE) LTD., *New Delhi*
PRENTICE-HALL OF JAPAN, INC., *Tokyo*

Handbook for
FRENCH COMPOSITION

DONALD STONE, JR.
Harvard University

PRENTICE-HALL, INC.   Englewood Cliffs, New Jersey

Second printing. . . . . August, 1965

Library of Congress Catalog Card No.: 65-15559

Printed in the United States of America

C-37270

Preface

This handbook is designed for a third-year college French course in which the instructor seeks to effect a transition from the language course to the literature level. In general, such courses consist of grammar review, extensive reading, and discussion of literary texts with numerous compositions. The intermediate stage has always been a difficult one for several reasons. A basic grammar book repeats second-year work; a sophisticated grammar is best used in a stylistic course and confuses the intermediate student who is only beginning to master the grammar fundamentals. For composition work, the students are still relying on translation and small, inadequate dictionaries. The resultant work abounds in *anglicismes*, shows quite indiscriminate use of the dictionary and a style that, at best, is a grammatically correct French, translated from the English. The purpose of this handbook is to meet as many of these problems as possible, within the context of the third year.

The handbook is divided into two sections. Section One contains expository material for problematic grammar points (Part I), vocabulary building and style (Part II), and difficulties in translation (Part III). Section Two contains, in addition to a series of exercises on the grammar lessons and a series of translation exercises, a further discussion of grammar and translation points that appear in the exercises (Appendix I and II). Finally, supplementary exercises are provided for teachers who wish to drill students on grammar and translation during the class hour.

While the table of contents suggests that the three parts of Section One—grammar, translation, and the dictionary—are rather separate and form a progression in work, they are, in fact, separated mainly for convenience; and in using the book, the teacher will readily discover that the exercises, whether grammar or translation, are constantly retesting the same material. Depending on the students' previous preparation, the teacher may either work as the material is presented (preferable if the group is particularly poor in writing) or alternate sections of grammar and translation (covering the dictionary material in conjunction with the translation exercises). These exercises have been so printed as to permit the student to see and learn from his own errors. In a typical three-hour week, students could be assigned one grammar discussion and the accompanying exercise for the first class. When he tears out his exercises, he will find underneath the English a suggested French translation, and, if he inserts a sheet of carbon paper before writing out his answer, his own translation. (The use of carbon paper could be at the discretion of the instructor, as the student will doubtless use scratch paper before vi writing out his final translation.) For the second class he could be assigned a study of the suggested French translation, an appreciation of his mistakes, and the discussion of further points in the appendix. Finally, he would take a test on the material during the third hour. (A similar procedure is possible for the translation passages.)

By calling this text a composition handbook, I have wanted to indicate at the outset that it is neither a grammar nor a dictionary nor a stylistic manual. In none of these areas does it claim to be complete. The length and coverage of the handbook are determined by the normal fifteen-week semester, but the most complete source of information on each aspect must be the individual instructor, who knows the needs and problems of his own students. For this same reason, I have chosen "handbook" over "workbook." The student's weekly composition remains the invaluable test of his progress and application; and I have wanted above all to define here the essential problems he will face and cover the most immediate solutions in a new and, hopefully, effective way.

I am indebted to J. D. Hubert, Librairie Plon, Editions Albin Michel, Cambridge University Press, Editions Denoel, and Librairie Gallimard for permission to quote from, respectively, *L'Esthétique des Fleurs du Mal;* J. Starobinski, *Jean-Jacques Rousseau, La Transparence et l'obstacle;* Henri Martineau, *L'Oeuvre de Stendhal;* F. C. Green, *The Mind of Proust;* Gonzague Truc, *Tableau du XXᵉ siècle, III: La Pensée;* and Marcel Proust, *A La Recherche du Temps Perdu.*

D. S., Jʀ.

Contents

ix

Handbook for

FRENCH COMPOSITION

 SECTION ONE

I Useful Techniques

1. GENDER

When facing the problem of gender, your first and surest reaction should be to use your dictionary. Here are some useful rules, however, to bear in mind:

Nouns ending in *-isme* are masculine: *le communisme, le romantisme.* . . .

Nouns ending in *-tion* are feminine: *la composition, la position.* . . .

Most nouns ending in *-ment* are masculine: *le changement, le mouvement* (But: *la jument.* . . .)

Most nouns ending in *-té* are feminine: *la beauté la bonté, la fidelité* (But: *le comité, le côté, le comté, un été.* . . .)

Note that the following nouns are always feminine, regardless of the gender of the person referred to: *la dupe, la connaissance* (*Il est une de mes connaissances*), *la personne, la victime* (*Louis XVI fut une victime de la révolution*).

3

Do not let certain peculiarities of pronunciation fool you. Note these phrases: *un nouvel avion, un bon exemple, le premier acte.* In each case the noun is masculine, but because of the phenomenon of liaison, the final consonant of the adjective is linked to the vowel of the noun, producing a pronunciation which is exactly like that of the feminine form of the adjective. In writing, however, you must strictly observe the gender of the noun, whatever the pronunciation may be.

Above all, do not make up rules. Students commonly consider all nouns ending in a mute *e* as being feminine. Nothing could be more false, e.g., *le poète, le poème, le système.* . . .

2. CE AND IL

The use of these pronouns is especially difficult, first because their use is a grammatical distinction, rarely a translation distinction, and secondly, because the pronouns appear in many different contexts that are often difficult to relate. For these reasons you should study very closely each of the various pairs of sentences that distinguish the use of the pronouns until you can appreciate and reproduce these distinctions. Naturally, if rules for usage are given, they should be memorized with the examples.

1. General Statements

Il est dans le bureau où il reçoit ses étudiants.
He is in the office where he receives his students.
C'est dans le bureau qu'il reçoit ses étudiants.
It is in the office that he receives his students.

C'est . . . *que* is a useful formula for emphasis. The sense of the sentence is best rendered: "He receives his students in the office" ("Not elsewhere" understood).

2. With Adjectives and Infinitives

C'est facile à dire.
It's (that's) easy to say.
Il est facile de dire cela.
It is easy to say that.

In this case there is a definite rule. If the infinitive has a direct object, the formula "*il* . . . + adjective + *de* + infinitive" must be used (cf. *de faire cela*). Otherwise you must use "*ce* . . . + adjective + *à.*"

4

3. Possession

A qui est ce chapeau?
Whose hat is it?

Il est à Paul.
It's Paul's.

Quel chapeau est-ce?
What hat is that?

C'est celui de Paul.
It's Paul's.

These constructions must be kept strictly separate. The pronouns *celui, celle,* etc., can be used only with *ce*. Note that despite the identity of translation, there is a slight difference in meaning, as the questions indicate. *Il est à Paul* is the true formula for possession. In the sentences with *ce*, the pronoun retains a certain demonstrative value. "It's Paul's" = "That's Paul's." Cf. also, "it's (that's) easy to say." (*C'est facile à dire.*)

4. With Nouns Indicating Profession, Citizenship, Religion, etc.

Il est médecin.
He's a doctor.

Il est excellent médecin.
He's an excellent doctor.

C'est un médecin.
He's a doctor.

C'est un excellent médecin.
He's an excellent doctor.

C'est le meilleur médecin de la ville.
He's the best doctor in the city.[1]

Notice first how useless it is to distinguish these constructions through their translation. Fortunately, the grammar rule here is quite simple. "He," "she" is rendered by *ce* only (1) if the noun is modified by the indefinite article or (2) if the adjective is in the superlative degree. Otherwise, the pronoun must be *il, elle*. For "they," the same rule applies, except that the deciding element is not the indefinite article *un, une,* but its plural form *des:*

Ils sont catholiques.
They are Catholic.

Ce sont des catholiques.
They are Catholic.

3. Y AND EN

It is traditional to define these two pronouns as replacing *à* + a noun and *de* + a noun, respectively. A further rule usually states that

---

[1] N.B. "in" with the superlative is translated by *de*.

these pronouns may not be used for persons,[2] in which case they are replaced by disjunctive pronouns, *elle, lui, elles, eux:*

Je serai à Paris cet été.
J'y serai.

Je m'intéresse à Napoléon.
Je m'intéresse à lui.

Je pense à mes parents.
Je pense à eux.

Je veux du pain.
J'en veux.

Je ne peux pas me passer de Marie.
Je ne peux pas me passer d'elle.

At the same time, you should be aware of a certain number of refinements on these rules which, though not difficult, can cause trouble.

I. A group of verbs—*obéir à, désobéir à, nuire à, succéder à, plaire à, survivre à, ressembler à,* etc.—with persons use the personal pronouns *lui, leur,* rather than the disjunctive construction of *à* or *de* plus pronoun.

Il obéit à son père.   Il plaît à Marie.
Il lui obéit.   Il lui plaît.

II. Since many verbs and expressions take *à* or *de* before a dependent infinitive, the pronouns *y* and *en* may also be used to replace infinitive phrases.

Il songeait à nous écrire.
Il y songeait.

Il avait peur de nous perdre de vue.
Il en avait peur.

If the verb is transitive, however, and the infinitive phrase represents a true direct object, the pronoun to be used is *le* and not *y* or *en.*

Il apprend à parler français.
Il l'apprend.

Il regrette de partir.
Il le regrette.

If you are not absolutely sure which kind of verb you are dealing with, a helpful guide is to transform the sentence into a question. If the question is formed with *qu'est-ce que*, the pronoun is *le;* if the question is formed with *à quoi* or *de quoi*, then *y* or *en* is used accordingly.

Qu'est-ce qu'il apprend?   Il apprend à parler français.
                             Il l'apprend.

6 *But:* A quoi songeait-il?   Il songeait à nous écrire.
                             Il y songeait.

---

[2] *En* may be used to refer to persons when referring to a group rather than to a single person, e.g., *Y a-t-il beaucoup de soldats en ville? Oui, j'en ai vu autour du café de la Paix.* (Notice that the past participle *never* agrees with *en.*)

De quoi avait-il peur?   Il avait peur de nous perdre de vue.
Il en avait peur.

4. AGREEMENT OF THE PAST PARTICIPLE

I. General rule: If the direct object precedes the auxiliary, the past participle agrees in number and gender with the direct object (*e* for feminine singular; *es* for feminine plural; *s* for masculine plural). There is no ending added in the case of masculine singular, however.

J'ai	vu	Marie.		Je	l'ai	vue.	
aux.	*p.p.*	*d.o.*			*d.o. aux.*	*p.p.*	

J'ai	vu	trois	chevaux.	Je	les	ai	vus.
aux.	*p.p.*		*d.o.*		*d.o.*	*aux.*	*p.p.*

II. The only exception to this rule is the case of the sixteen intransitive verbs (*venir, aller, mourir,* etc.) conjugated with *être*. In sentences with these verbs, the past participle agrees with the subject: Marie est partie. Nous sommes entrés.

Problems

I. The relative pronoun *que*.

Many students fail to realize that this pronoun, whose function in the clause is that of a direct object, can also affect the past participle, depending on its antecedent.

Je préfère la robe rouge que vous avez portée hier soir.
          antecedent   d.o.   aux. p.p.

II. The reflexive pronouns *me, te, se, nous, vous*.

As these pronouns can be either direct or indirect objects, you must be careful to determine the function of the pronoun to decide whether or not there will be any past participle agreement.

Cf. Marie a dit: je me suis beaucoup amusée hier.

Marie a dit: je me suis lavé les cheveux hier.

In the first sentence, *me* is a direct object, hence the agreement *amusée*. In the second sentence, the *me* is the indirect object, *cheveux* is the direct object, so no agreement is possible. It might be helpful to remember that in certain reflexive expressions, e.g., *se plaindre de, se rendre compte de, s'imaginer,* the reflexive pronoun is *never* a direct object. Elles s'en sont *rendu* compte. Nous nous en sommes *plaint*.

III. Intransitive verbs that become transitive.

Among the sixteen intransitive verbs conjugated with *être*, certain may be used transitively, e.g., *rentrer* (to take in), *sortir* (to take out), *monter* (to go up, to take up), *descendre* (to go down, to take down),

7

etc. In this instance they are conjugated with *avoir* and follow the general rule.

Ils sont descendus.
They went downstairs.

Ils ont descendu les malles.
They took the trunks downstairs.

Ils les ont descendues.
They took them downstairs.

5. THE PARTITIVE

There is probably no more fundamental concept of French so little understood and so incorrectly handled by English-speaking students than the partitive. It is difficult to use because it is difficult to define in terms of an English equivalent and is best appreciated through an examination of its use in French. First consider these sentences:

1. Il aime le vin.
   He likes wine.
2. Il boit du vin.
   He is drinking wine.
3. Il aime les femmes.
   He likes women.
4. Il a vu des femmes dans la rue.
   He saw women in the street.

In sentences 1 and 3, the noun has no quantitative value and the definite article is used. In sentences 2 and 4, the noun denotes a quantity, an amount of wine, a number of women. Because of this quantitative value, the definite article is replaced by the partitive.

Observations

1. The root of the partitive is the expression of quantity with a noun whose meaning is left general (wine vs. *the* wine of the last harvest; women vs. *the* women he first saw at the railroad station).
2. While the word "some" might be supplied before the nouns in sentences 2 and 4, there is no real translation clue to the partitive; it must be recognized through its definition.
3. The partitive is formed by using *de* + the definite article *le, la, l'*. Do not forget that *de* + *le* forms *du*. *De* + *les*, of course, is *des*.

Peculiarities

The partitive becomes *de, d'* in three cases.

1. If the sentence is negative: *Il boit du vin. Il ne boit pas de vin.*

8

2. If an adjective precedes a plural noun: *Il a vu des femmes dans la rue.*
   Il a vu de jolies femmes dans la rue.
3. With adverbs of quantity or nouns of quantity:[1] *Il boit du vin. Il boit une bouteille de vin par jour. Il a vu des femmes dans la rue. Il a vu beaucoup de femmes dans la rue.*

Other Peculiarities

1. If a noun which would normally be preceded by the partitive is in some way modified so that the idea of quantity passes from a general to a specific case, the partitive rules no longer apply.

1. Il boit du vin blanc.
   He is drinking white wine.
2. Il boit du vin d'Alsace.
   He is drinking Alsatian wine.
3. Il ne boit plus du vin que Marie lui a acheté.
   He no longer drinks any of the wine that Mary bought him.
4. Il ne parle plus des films qu'il a vus à Paris.
   He no longer talks about the films he saw in Paris.

Since in sentences 3 and 4 the idea of quantity is clearly restricted (the wine *Mary bought,* the films *he saw*), the partitive disappears and although the sentences are negative, *du* and *des,* not *de* appear before the noun. In 1 and 2 no such restriction is present, and were they to be put in the negative, the partitive rules would apply: *Il ne boit pas de vin d'Alsace.*

2. This distinction is also observed in that large category of verbs used with *de,* e.g., *avoir besoin de, se passer de,* etc.

If the noun is plural [2] and not specific as defined above, *de* is used:
Je ne me passerai jamais de cigarettes.
I shall never do without cigarettes.

But, become specific, the noun is preceded by *des:*

Je ne me passerai jamais des cigarettes que j'ai commencé à fumer en Egypte.
I shall never do without the cigarettes I began smoking in Egypt.

3. A final application of this principle can be found in the construction

---

[1] Note these exceptions: *bien des* (many), *la plupart des* (most). *Il a vu bien des femmes dans la rue. La plupart* must be used with caution. It is always used with a plural noun (except *la plupart du temps*) and a plural verb: *La plupart des hommes sont heureux.* With a noun in the singular, you must use *la plus grande partie: la plus grande partie de la classe.* . . .

[2] With a singular noun the negation has no effect upon the expression of quantity. I need a cigarette. *J'ai besoin d'une cigarette.* I don't need a cigarette. *Je n'ai pas besoin d'une cigarette.*

of two nouns joined by "of" (*de*). Again, if the noun following the *de* is unmodified as defined above, the *de* is invariable:

une paire de manches
a pair of sleeves

son choix de femmes
his choice of women

But: La sélection des ministres à remplacer a duré plusieurs jours.
The choice of the ministers to be replaced lasted several days.

Note that in these three cases there is a certain translation aid—the "of the" which appears before the modified nouns. The analysis should show you, however, that the problem is basically grammatical and you should treat it as such.

6. SUBJUNCTIVE

1. Use

In previous study of the subjunctive, you have doubtlessly encountered a list of categories such as the following: fear, doubt, emotion, desire, probability, necessity, hypothesis, etc. complemented by miscellaneous categories such as *croire, penser,* and *espérer,* impersonal expressions and subordinate conjunctions, all of which contain certain exemplary forms that require the subjunctive.

Speaking of the subjunctive by categories is not only useful, it fulfills the important function of making you appreciate its value in contrast to the indicative. The subjunctive is the mode of subjectivity—what the speaker feels, wants, supposes—while the indicative is the mode of objectivity, expressing what is objectively true. It is the difference between *Je doute qu'il vienne,* I doubt he'll come (the subjunctive because the speaker has made a subjective analysis of the situation) and *Il est venu à l'heure,* He came on time (the indicative because we are dealing with an objective fact). On the other hand, presenting the subjunctive by categories also involves many problems, not the least of which, as the miscellaneous categories above suggest, is that the subjunctive is used in many instances which do not fall conveniently into the large categories. Moreover, thinking of the subjunctive in these terms often leads to an abuse of the mode in contexts where nothing justifies its use. A favorite use of the subjunctive among third-year students is with *croire—Je crois qu'il vienne,* I think he may come—where the justification is the indication of doubt, a bona fide subjunctive category, when, in truth, *croire* requires the subjunctive *only* if used negatively or interrogatively: *Croyez-vous qu'il vienne.* The easiest and the surest solution to this situation is to learn not the categories, but the forms which require the subjunctive. It is far more important to know that *tenir à* requires the subjunctive than to remember emotion and necessity, as neither case covers this very common use of the subjunctive.

We list below the most common forms which are followed by the subjunctive. If you master these forms and can do the exercises correctly, you have mastered the essentials of the subjunctive.

A. Verbs

désirer que

vouloir que

souhaiter que

tenir à ce que

exiger que

défendre que

aimer mieux que

préférer que

douter que

être triste (content, heureux, surpris) que

regretter que

prendre garde que

craindre que

avoir peur que

B. Impersonal Constructions

il semble que

il faut que

il importe que

il vaut mieux que

il convient que

il se peut que

c'est dommage que

il est nécessaire que

il est important que

il est convenable que

il est normal que

il est juste que

il est faux que

il est possible que

il est bon que

il est essentiel que

il est impossible que

il est rare que

il est préférable que

C. Subordinate Conjunctions

avant que

en attendant que

jusqu'à ce que

afin que

pour que

de sorte que

pourvu que

sans que

à moins que

de crainte que

de peur que

quoique

bien que

D. Relative Clauses

(1) with the superlatives: e.g.

$$c'est\ le\ seul \begin{cases} qui.\ .\ .\ . \\ que.\ .\ .\ . \end{cases}$$

$$c'est\ le\ meilleur \begin{cases} qui.\ .\ .\ . \\ que.\ .\ .\ . \end{cases}$$

$$c'est\ le\ plus\ beau \begin{cases} qui.\ .\ .\ . \\ que.\ .\ .\ . \end{cases}$$

(2) with indefinite antecedent: e.g.

il n'y a rien que. . . .
je cherche un homme qui. . . .
connaissez-vous un livre qui. . . .
qui que. . . .
quoi que. . . .
quel que. . . .
quelque. . . . que. . . .
si. . . . que. . . .

2. Forms

The subjunctive is no more difficult to form than any other tense. Far fewer verbs are irregular in the subjunctive; however, as forming the present and imperfect subjunctive is predicated on knowing other forms of the verb, you should use this opportunity to review not only the rules for the formation of the subjunctive, but also your general knowledge of the verb forms involved.

Present subjunctive: The present subjunctive is formed from the third-person plural of the present indicative minus the personal ending *-ent.*

ils parlent—que je parle	ils comprennent—que je comprenne
ils partent—que je parte	ils craignent—que je craigne
ils courent—que je coure	ils boivent—que je boive

The following verbs are irregular in the present subjunctive:

avoir—que j'aie	pourvoir—que je puisse
être—que je sois	vouloir—que je veuille
aller—que j'aille	valoir—que je vaille
faire—que je fasse	falloir—qu'il faille
savoir—que je sache	

In verbs like *battre* and *vivre,* do not confuse the present indicative (*je bats, je vis*) with the present subjunctive (*que je batte, que je vive*). Notice also that the endings are the same for all verbs (*e, es, e, ions, iez, ent*) except *avoir* and *être:*

que j'aie	que je sois
que tu aies	que tu sois
qu'il ait	qu'il soit
que nous ayons	que nous soyons
que vous ayez	que vous soyez
qu'ils aient	qu'ils soient

Finally, note that *aller,* like *avoir* and *être,* has a different stem in the first and second person plural (*que j'aille, que nous allions*).

Present perfect subjunctive: The present subjunctive of the auxiliary (*être* or *avoir*) with the past participle.

que j'aie fini   que je sois allé

Imperfect subjunctive: The imperfect subjunctive is formed from the past definite minus the personal ending.

aller	j'allai	*stem* all-
faire	je fis	*stem* fi-
mourir	je mourus	*stem* mouru-

To the stem are added (1) for the first conjugation (all verbs with infinitive ending -*er*)

asse
asses
ât
assions
assiez
assent

(2) for all other conjugations

sse
sses
ˆt
ssions
ssiez
ssent

Note that as the personal ending is the same in the third person singular for both the past definite and the imperfect subjunctive for all verbs not of the first conjugation, you must be careful not to confuse these two tenses in your compositions. The imperfect subjunctive adds a circumflex to the vowel preceding the personal ending.

faire   *past definite:* il fit   *imperfect subjunctive:* il fît
mourir   *past definite:* il mourut   *imperfect subjunctive:* il mourût

Pluperfect subjunctive: The imperfect subjunctive of the auxiliary (*être* or *avoir*) with the past participle.

qu'il eût fini   qu'il fût allé

7.   SEQUENCE OF TENSES

Sequence of tenses is much more flexible in English than in French. Therefore, while you can often keep in French the tenses of English, you must always be careful to recognize those instances in French where the sequence is rigidly defined.

1.   Conditional Sentences

Here are three patterns for conditional sentences in French:

1. *Si* with the present + future: Si je pars, il partira. (*If I leave, he'll leave.*)
2. *Si* with the imperfect + conditional: Si je partais, il partirait. (*If I left, he'd leave.*)

3. *Si* with the pluperfect + past conditional: Si j'étais parti, il serait parti. (*If I had left, he would have left.*)

Part of the explanation for this rigid pattern here and in other examples is that to use other sequences often changes the meaning. For example, it is possible to use this combination: *Si* with the present + present, *si* with the imperfect + imperfect.

S'il pleut, je porte un imperméable. *If it rains, I wear a raincoat.*
Si elle le grondait, il pleurait. *If she scolded him, he cried.*

However, in neither case is *si* a conditional *si*, but rather means "whenever" (Whenever she scolded him. . . .) and indicates habitual action.

2. The Future with Temporal Conjunctions

With *quand, lorsque, dès que,* and *aussitôt que,* if the main verb of the sentence is in the future or an imperative, the verb of the subordinate clause must be future or future perfect.

Aussitôt que vous le *verrez, dites-lui* de me téléphoner.
As soon as you see him, tell him to call me.

Il nous *rendra* visite dès qu'il *sera* de retour.
He'll visit us as soon as he comes back.

Aussitôt que *j'aurai* terminé mon travail, je *pourrai* répondre.
As soon as I have finished my work, I can answer.

Note how in each case the English gives no indication of the verb construction used in French.

3. Peculiarities of Literary Style

1. *Passé Simple (Passé défini)*: As you may know, the past definite is reserved today for literary style and is not used in conversation, where it is replaced by the past indefinite (passé composé), since the basic function of both tenses is the same, i.e. to express a single event begun and completed in the past. The sentence: *Il descendit dans la rue et puis il traversa la place,* would in conversation be expressed, *Il est descendu dans la rue et puis il a traversé la place.*

At the same time you should take pains not to confuse either tense with the imperfect. The imperfect by virtue of its function—to express condition, habitual action, or action begun in the past and continuing to a specific time in the past—cannot be replaced by any other tense and therefore appears in conversation and literary style. This sentence: *Il lisait quand le téléphone sonna,* would in conversation occasion but *one* change: *Il lisait quand le téléphone a sonné.*

2. *Subjunctive:* You should know that in modern French the imperfect and pluperfect subjunctive are used only in literary style. In conversation they are replaced by the present and passé composé of the subjunc-

14

tive, respectively. Thus, while an author would write: *Il aurait voulu qu'elle lui dît la vérité avant qu'elle n'eût quitté Paris,* he would say: *Il aurait voulu qu'elle lui dise la vérité avant qu'elle n'ait quitté Paris.*

3. *Past Perfect:* With temporal conjunctions and the English past perfect, a variety of tenses may be used in French.

(*a*) In literary style, the sequence is past anterior and past definite:
Lorsque le roi eut dîné, il envoya chercher les danseuses.
When the king had dined, he sent for the dancing girls.

(*b*) In conversation, use a supercomposed past and the past indefinite (the combination pluperfect and past indefinite is also used):
Lorsque le roi a eu dîné, il a envoyé chercher les danseuses.
        (avait)
When the king had dined, he sent for the dancing girls.

(*c*) In conversation or literary style, if the sentence indicates habitual action, the sequence is pluperfect and imperfect:
Lorsque le roi avait dîné, il envoyait chercher les danseuses.
When the king had dined, he would send for the dancing girls.

Note this sentence could also be translated: *Whenever the king had dined, he sent (used to send) for the dancing girls.*

8.   ORTHOGRAPHIC DIFFERENCES

Despite the large number of words which are spelled alike in English and French, there are many French words which resemble English and yet receive a slightly different spelling. These words must be carefully memorized and contrasted with English.

ENGLISH	FRENCH
address	adresse (F.)
aggressive	agressif
apartment	appartement (M.)
appearance	apparence (F.)
authority	autorité (F.)
character	caractère (M.)
characteristic	caractéristique
civilization	civilisation (F.)
cf. also, organization	organisation (F.)
comfortable	confortable
committee	comité (M.)
correspondence	correspondance (F.)
cf. also, independence	indépendance (F.)
desire	désir (M.)
develop	développer

development	développement (M.)
dinner	dîner (M.)
eccentric	excentrique
ecstasy	extase (F.)
enemy	ennemi (M.) — 20
enthusiasm	enthousiasme (M.)
exaggerate	exagérer
example	exemple (M.)
exercise	exercice (M.)
form	forme (F.)
guard	garde (M.)
homage	hommage (M.)
impressionism	impressionnisme (M.)
individual (noun)	individu (M.)
language	langage (M.) — 30
license	licence (F.)
lyricism	lyrisme (M.)
manner	manière (F.)
marriage	mariage (M.)
marry	marier
mechanism	mécanisme (M.)
medicine	médecine (F.)
melancholy	mélancolie (F.)
negligible	négligeable
object	objet (M.) — 40
ornament	ornement (M.)
personage	personnage (M.)
personal	personnel
personality	personnalité (F.)
realize	réaliser
reflection	réflexion (F.)
resemble	ressembler
responsible	responsable
romanticism	romantisme (M.)
rhyme	rime (F.) — 50
rhythm	rythme (M.)
sense	sens (M.)
syllable	syllabe (F.)
symmetry	symétrie (F.)
throne	trône (M.)
universe	univers (M.)
16 verb	verbe (M.)
virtue	vertu (F.) — 58

9. Orthographic Changes

1. The Influence of the Mute *e*

Three categories of verbs (all first conjugation) are affected by this phenomenon.

1. *-e* + consonant + *er* (*lever, appeler, jeter*)
2. *-é* + consonant + *er* (*préférer, espérer*)
3. *-yer* (*nettoyer, essuyer*)

While the form of change varies, the principles involved are always the same: whenever the *-e*, *-é* + consonant or the *-y* is followed by a mute (unaccented) *e*, a change in spelling must occur. Thus: We write *nous appelons, je jetai, vous espérez* (here though the "e" is unaccented, it is pronounced as *é* and not considered mute); but before the mute *e*—

for verbs like *lever*, a grave accent must be added: je lève, j'achèterai;
for *jeter* and *appeler*, the consonant is doubled: ils jetteront, tu t'appelles;
for verbs like *espérer*, the acute accent becomes a grave: il préfère, ils espèrent.[1] For verbs like *nettoyer*, the y becomes *i:* je nettoie, nous essuierons.

2. Soft *c* and *g*

In verbs like *commencer* and *manger* the soft sound of the *c* and *g* must be maintained throughout the conjugation. Thus, before any verb ending which begins with *a, o,* or *u,* a spelling change occurs.

Verbs ending in *-cer* add a cedilla to the *c:* nous commencerons, *but:* nous commençons.

Verbs ending in *-ger* add the letter *e* before the ending: je mange, *but:* mangeant, nous mangeons. . . .

3. Miscellany

1. *Connaître, paraître.* These verbs keep the circumflex.
   (a) in the present tense in the third person singular only: il, elle, on connaît;
   (b) in the future and conditional throughout: il connaîtra, nous connaîtrions. . . .
2. *Apercevoir.* This irregular verb maintains a soft *c* by adding a cedilla when necessary: j'aperçois, ils aperçoivent. . . .

---

[1] For verbs like *espérer*, NO change occurs before the future or conditional ending, however: *nous espérerons*.

II Facing the Problem of Composition

1. TESTING YOUR VOCABULARY

The intermediate college language course is a crucial period in the development of your mastery of written French. You have been guided for some time in your writing by grammar and translation exercises. Now you must learn to apply the skills so obtained in a completely creative context—the literary composition. Often the habit of translation is so firmly engrained in a student that he will write his composition in English and then translate it. From the beginning you must realize that translation cannot lead to such a mastery. You should begin now, if you have not done so, to acquire new skills and find new sources of information other than the dictionary.

Besides your teacher, your greatest aid to composition is your reading. Undoubtedly your reading will be varied and the value of the text will change in accordance with the style of the author. But whatever the text, its value as a source of constructions and vocabulary should never be overlooked. From the first day of your third-year course, you should keep a notebook for corrections on your compositions and words and useful constructions met in your reading. By "useful" we do not mean every unfamiliar word or phrase you encounter, but the turn of phrase, the expressive word that cannot be obtained through translation.

Read through carefully the following texts, one of literary criticism, the other a passage from Proust, which have been translated into English. Whenever you meet an underlined word or expression, translate it into French in the space provided.

Extreme variableness does not imply that the mind is _____ in a state of conflict. The protean Rousseau of the *Persifleur*, the infinitely variable Jean-Jacques of the Dialogues, live through _____ a succession of dissimilar moments; but in each of these moments they cling to themselves, if only long enough _____ to feel the sudden upsurge _____ of a new aspect of the self. They submit to this change as if it were a law imposed upon them. They are not the masters of their metamorphoses. They change as does the sky. They are satisfied _____ to take part in their metamorphosis without revolting against it.

Likewise, too, no more than the seasons to its flowerless _____ arms stretching into the sea, do modern times bring any change to the Gothic city; I knew it, I could not imagine it, but that is what I wanted to gaze upon with the same desire which long ago, when I was a boy _____, in the very ardor of departure, had broken and robbed me of the strength _____ to make the journey, I longed to find myself face to face with my Venetian imaginings, to observe how that divided sea held in the clutches _____ of its meanderings, like the sinuosities of the ocean stream, an urban and sophisticated civilization . . .

Now compare your version with the original, first of Starobinski:

L'extrême variabilité n'implique pas que la conscience se trouve en état de conflit. Le Rousseau protée du *Persifleur*, le Jean-Jacques infiniment variable des *Dialogues* vivent une succession d'instants dissemblables, mais en chacun de ces instants ils adhèrent à eux-mêmes, ne fût-ce que le temps de sentir survenir un nouvel aspect du moi. Ils subissent ce changement comme une loi qui leur serait imposée. Ils ne sont pas les maîtres de leurs métamorphoses. Ils changent comme le ciel change . . . Ils se contentent d'assister à leur métamorphose, sans insurger contre elle.

"Is in a state" doubtlessly became *est* . . . ; "are satisfied," *sont contents*. In both cases Starobinski rejects the colorless and overworked verb "*être*" for other possibilities. Learning substitute expressions for *être* and *faire* will give an immediate variety to your style.

The entire phrase "if only long enough to feel the sudden upsurge . . ." should be a warning to students who feel translations can suffice to produce a good French style. Without the construction *ne fût-ce que*, you inevitably fell into some cumbersome circumlocution that cries translation. Likewise, unless you were familiar with *survenir*—to appear suddenly, unexpectedly—you rendered noun for noun and lost the grammatical smoothness and lexical precision of *sentir survenir*. Finally, did you use a preposition after *vivre* for "live through"? Here it is as important to learn new constructions with familiar verbs as to learn unfamiliar terms for the first time.

While no one expects the intermediate student to write like Proust, it is scarcely undesirable to strive for an active appreciation of his vocabulary. Again test yourself through the original:

Aussi bien, pas plus que les saisons à ses bras de mer infleurissables, les modernes années n'apportent point de changement à la cité gothique; je le savais, je ne pouvais l'imaginer, ou l'imaginant, voilà ce que je voulais, de ce même désir qui jadis, quand j'étais enfant, dans l'ardeur même du départ, avait brisé en moi la force de partir: me trouver face à face avec mes imaginations vénitiennes; contempler comment cette mer divisée enserrait de ses méandres, comme les replis du fleuve Océan, une civilisation urbaine et raffinée. . . .*

Did "flowerless" become *sans fleurs,* "held in the clutches," *tenait dans les griffes?* Was it a surprise to see *enfant* and not *garçon* for "when I was a boy"? You should appreciate as well the simple elegance of *avait brisé en moi la force de partir* which replaces the desultory "broken and robbed me of the strength to make the journey."

Each indication should prove to you graphically how invaluable, and necessary, a strong vocabulary can be. The difference between *sans fleurs* and *infleurissables, tenait dans les griffes* and *enserrait* is the definition of that gap between translation from English and French composition. The latter forms, like *sentir survenir*, are not only more French, they are more expressive, far richer, for the meaning, as happens so often in French, is concentrated in one word and not dissipated among several. No teacher can be expected to extract from the dictionary all these terms. The exercises and the reference dictionary included here are to help you overcome the most immediate problems with vocabulary faced by a third-year student and should be thoroughly studied. But this is only the beginning, and your vocabulary will grow only if you yourself make the effort.

2. A Word about Style

Just as the pronunciation of French requires the English-speaking student to change certain habits, French stylistics demand a definite reorientation on the part of the non-French student. There is an old cliché about French—"What isn't clear, isn't French." This clarity has certain stylistic underpinnings, the most notable of which is a strong reliance on coordinate constructions (*mais, et, ou,* etc.) where English dotes on sub-

* Marcel Proust, *A La Recherche du temps perdu* (Paris: Editions Gallimard, 1919), vol. XII, pp. 260-61.

ordination ("when," "since," "although," etc.). Students writing in French often obscure their expression by reproducing in their compositions this tendency toward elaborate subordination and allowing sentences to grow to unintelligible proportions. To counteract this, avoid the use of several subordinate conjunctions or relative pronouns within a single sentence.

Consider this passage of French where coordinate constructions are italicized and subordinate ones in boldface type:

La politique, la religion *bien plus que* l'art purement littéraire demeurent son souci. Il y apporte la force *et* la souplesse d'une intelligence non prévenue, *et* il réclame le droit, pour le philosophe, de se tenir aux méthodes philosophiques sans se contraindre par une trop stricte érudition. Nous voudrions, dit-il, à propos d'excès de ce genre de M. Couchod, "nous vourions y éplinger quelques observations sur une tendance commune à la plupart des exégètes inspirés du pur esprit philosophique *ou* historiques, *et* **qui** consiste à faire de l'histoire *ou* de la philologie la mesure des êtres *ou* des choses . . ." Animé de cet esprit de mesure **que** n'abandonnent *ni* l'esprit critique *ni* une ironie incisive *mais* bien plaisante il fait le tour des hommes *et* des idées d'aujourd'hui.*

Within the entire passage there is not a single subordinate conjunction and only two relative pronouns. On the other hand, coordinate constructions abound. Through the coordinate structure, the essence of each group of ideas is contained in the principal parts of the clauses. The ideas follow smoothly, in a linear pattern, with amplitude provided primarily through carefully chosen adjectives. When the syntax is more complex, as in the second clause of the second sentence, the smooth movement of ideas is assured by the natural progression of constructions—(*le droit, pour . . . de*) (*se tenir aux . . .*) (*sans*) (*se contraindre par . . .*). This tightness of construction prevails even to the end, where the author begins not with a subordinate conjunction, but with a past participle directly dependent on the subject. If you find your sentences growing long and involved, be sure you can schematize the progression of ideas in this way. If you can't, the sentence should be broken up and reworded.

You may feel that this passage alone cannot suffice to establish a norm. But even if we return to the Starobinski passage, where subordinate constructions are more numerous, you should be able, nevertheless, to appreciate the resultant clarity and its relationship to the sentence structure. Here is the text again with coordinate conjunctions in italics and subordinate constructions in boldface type:

L'extrême variabilité n'implique pas **que** la conscience se trouve en état de conflit. Le Rousseau protée du *Persifleur*, le Jean-Jacques infiniment variable des *Dialogues* vivent une succession d'instants dissemblables, *mais* en chacun de ces instants ils adhèrent à eux-mêmes, ne **fut-ce** que le temps de sentir survenir un nouvel aspect du moi. Ils subissent ce changement comme une loi **que** serait imposée. Ils ne sont pas les maîtres de leurs métamorphoses. Ils changent

21

* Gonzague Truc, *Tableau du XXᵉ siècle, III La Pensée* (Paris: Denoël, 1933), pp. 145-46.

comme le vent change . . . Ils se contentent d'assister à leur métamorphose, sans s'insurger contre elle.

It is immediately clear that, numerically speaking, the subordinate constructions dominate. Yet they do not account for the greatest part of the amplitude of this passage. For while there is only one coordinate conjunction, *"mais,"* the compound subject of the second sentence and the string of short sentences at the end account for an equal portion of the passage. Moreover, the subordination is discreet (never more than one construction per sentence) and above all is so distributed as to achieve a fine balance between length of the sentence and the exposition of ideas in short, well-knit syntactical groups.

A number of translation exercises are provided in Section II to give you further practice in learning to write correct, idiomatic French. The first two exercises are intended primarily to test your ability to use a number of French expressions that are frequently sources of trouble to English-speaking students. If you are not sure of your translation, refer to the dictionary in Part III. When you have completed your translation and your teacher allows you to examine the sample French provided, you will notice certain numbers in parentheses throughout the text. They refer to the entries in the reference dictionary and will guide you to an explanation of most of the translation pitfalls contained in the text. Footnote numbers refer you to Appendix II. Here you will find supplementary material explaining grammatical and stylistic peculiarities not presented in the grammar section. Exercises III-V, as they are examples of original French prose, are intended to provide you, in a context of increasing difficulty, with the opportunity to reproduce as nearly as possible a modern critical French style. As with the selections just analyzed, note the vocabulary and the sentence structure and apply what you have learned here to your own compositions.

III A Reference Dictionary

1. Achieve

Achever means "to complete" never "to achieve"; e.g., *Rousseau est mort sans achever* Les Rêveries. "Achieve" is best translated according to the context.

Elle l'aida à atteindre son but.
She helped him achieve his goal.

Napoléon remporta maintes victoires avant sa défaite.
Napoleon achieved many a victory before defeat.

Il pense qu'il peut arriver à tout faire.
He thinks he can achieve anything.

Il a obtenu un succès sans égal.
He achieved unequaled success.

2. Act (verb)

Note the difference between *agir* ("to act") and *s'agir de* ("to be a question of"):

> Il a attendu trop longtemps pour agir.
> *He waited too long to act.*

> Dans *Adolphe* il s'agit d'une liaison qui survit à l'amour des partenaires.
> Adolphe *is the story of* (*literally, in* Adolphe *it is a question of*) *a liaison which outlives the couple's love.*

Note that whatever the translation, *s'agir de* is an impersonal construction and the only possible subject is *il*.

3. Actual(ly)

"Actual," meaning "real" is translated *réel* or *véritable;* "actually" is translated by *réellement, véritablement, en fait, en vérité.*

> Il dit qu'il était malade; en fait il se portait très bien.
> *He said he was sick; actually he was quite well.*

> Elle nous a toujours caché ce qui était sa condition véritable.
> *She always hid from us what her actual condition was.*

Actuel in French means "present"; *actuellement* means "at the present time." It may never be used to translate "actual" as defined above.

> Le président actuel de la France est De Gaulle.
> *De Gaulle is the present President of France.*

4. Affect

"Affect" can be translated in French by *affecter* only in the sense of "assume," "take on": *affecter une forme, affecter une manière.*

"Affect" in the sense of "influence," "touch," must be translated in terms of the precise nuance of the context:

> Ses mots me touchèrent profondément.
> *His words affected (touched) me deeply.*

> La loi nous intéresse tous.
> *The law affects (applies to) us all.*

> Ses mots influeront sur leur décision.
> *His words will affect (influence) their decision.*

> Son travail a altéré sa santé.
> *His work has affected (altered) his health.*

5. After

Do not confuse *après,* which is a preposition (*après le dîner*—after the dinner) with *après que,* which is the subordinate conjunction:

> Après qu'il eut dîné, il partit.
> *After he had dined, he left.*
> Cf. likewise: sans—*preposition*   sans que—*conjunction*
>   pour—*preposition*   pour que—*conjunction*
>   avant—*preposition*   avant que—*conjunction*

6. Agree

Never translate "agree" by *agréer.*
"To agree" (be in agreement) is *être d'accord, penser comme.*

> Nous sommes d'accord.   Il pense comme moi.
> *We agree.*

"To agree" (come to an agreement) is *tomber d'accord, se mettre d'accord.*

> Ils se mirent d'accord finalement sur une force de frappe indépendante.
> *They agreed at last about an independent striking force.*

7. All of the

The adjective *tout* means "all of." Never use *de* after this adjective.

> On a abattu tous les arbres.
> *All of the trees were cut down.*

8. As

Note these possibilities for translating "as":
"As" (comparison)—*comme:*

> Faites comme moi.
> *Do as I do.*

"As" (because of)—*comme, parce que:*

> Comme il n'avait pas d'argent, il. . . .
> *As he had no money, he. . . .*

"As" (when)—*au moment où:*

> Je parlais à son mari au moment où elle est entrée.
> *I was talking to her husband as she came in.*

"As" (progression)—(*au fur et*) *à mesure que:*

> Au fur et à mesure que les jours passaient, elle perdait tout espoir.
> *As the days passed, she lost all hope.*

9. Audience (in a theatre, etc.)

Never use *audience* to translate the English word "audience." *Audience* means "a hearing" or "audience" in the sense "to grant someone an audience."

Use, rather, *les spectateurs, l'auditoire* for a theatre; *les auditeurs* for a concert; *l'assistance* for a meeting. Note also:

> Toute la salle avait l'air de s'ennuyer.
> *The entire audience seemed bored.*

10. Because

Do not confuse *parce que* and *car*. They may both be translated by "because," but *parce que* has the sense of "for the reason that." *Car* means "for indeed," "in point of fact."

> Cf. Ne pleurez pas parce que je vais partir.   (*because*)
> Ne pleurez pas, car je vais partir.   (*for*)

11. Before

Avant, devant, and *auparavant* all mean "before," but they are not synonymous.

Avant is a preposition used to mean "before" in a temporal context.

> Son train est arrivé avant le mien.
> *His train arrived before mine.*

Devant is "before" (in front of) and is also a preposition.

> Elle passe toute sa journée devant le fourneau.
> *She spends all day before the stove.*

Auparavant is the adverb "before."

> J'avais fait sa connaissance auparavant.
> *I had met him before.*

12. By (a certain time)

"By" with expressions of time is best translated by *avant* and never *par*.

> Soyez de retour avant midi.
> *Be back by noon.*

13. Capable

"Capable" in the sense of "competent" is translated *compétent*.

> C'est un linguiste très compétent.
> *He is a very capable linguist.*

"Capable" meaning "able to do" is *capable de*.

> Il est capable de tout.
> *He is capable of anything.*

14. Capture

"Capture" in the sense of "seize" is best rendered by *prendre*.

> Après une longue bataille, ils ont pris la ville.
> *After a long battle, they captured the city.*

Arrêter, s'emparer de may be used to translate the verb in the sense of "arrest."

> Il a fallu une semaine seulement pour s'emparer du criminal.
> *It took only a week to capture the criminal.*

15. Change

The verb "change" when meaning to exchange one thing for another is always followed by *de*:

> Il a changé de train.
> *He changed trains.*

> Il a changé de chemise.
> *He changed his shirt.*

> Il a changé sa chaise de place.
> *He changed the position of his chair.*

But:

> Il a changé son billet de banque.
> *He changed a bank note.*

16. Character

The "character of a play, a novel, etc. is *le personnage;*

> Hamlet est un personnage complexe.
> *Hamlet is a complex character.*

Note also: main character—*le personnage principal*
minor character—*le personnage secondaire*

"Character" meaning "personality traits" is *le caractère:*

> Il a un caractère difficile.   ˙
> *He has a difficult character.*

17. Come (to a conclusion)

"Come" in this phrase is always translated *arriver:*

> Ils sont arrivés à des conclusions différentes.
> *They came to different conclusions.*

18. Concern

"Concern" may be translated by *concerner* in only one instance:

Cela ne vous concerne pas.
This does not concern you.

Otherwise use *s'intéresser à* (for people), *traiter de, s'agir de* (for plays, books, etc.).

Ce livre traite du problème . . .
This book is concerned with the problem . . .

Je ne m'y intéresse pas.
I am not concerned with that.

NB *se concerner avec* as a translation of "to be concerned with" *does not exist.*

19. Connection

Connexion in French is a technical term which can rarely if ever be used to translate the English word "connection." For a suitable translation study these examples:

Il y a un rapport évident entre ses sentiments et son style.
There is an evident connection between his feelings and his style.

Il est difficile d'établir des rapports entre ces faits.
It is difficult to establish a connection between these facts.

Ils ont cessé (rompu) toutes relations avec sa famille.
They have broken all connection with his family.

20. Criticism

"Criticism" is *la critique,* which should not be confused with *le critique,* meaning "critic."

21. Crucial

"Crucial" is best translated by *décisif* or *critique.*

Cette scène représente un moment décisif dans la pièce.
This scene is a critical (crucial) moment in the play.

22. Cut (a course)

"To cut" a course is translated *sécher une classe* or *s'absenter.*

Il a séché trop de classes ce semestre.
Il s'est absenté trop souvent ce semestre.
He has cut this course too often this semester.

28

23. Death

"Death" is *la mort*. Do not confuse this form with *la morte*, which means "a dead woman" or *le mort*, which means "a dead man."

> Cf. On sentait la mort partout, et le champ de bataille était couvert de morts.
> *You could smell death everywhere, and the battlefield was littered with the dead.*

24. Degree

Notice these possible translations of "degree":

> Il a détesté son travail à tel point que . . .
> *He hated his work to such a degree that . . .*
>
> On lui a demandé combien de grades il avait.
> *He was asked how many degrees he had.*
>
> Dans une certaine mesure, il était notre meilleur professeur.
> *To a certain degree he was our best professor.*

25. Effective

In its sense of "effectual," "effective" is translated *efficace*.

> Ses idées n'étaient pas efficaces.
> *His ideas were not effective.*

In a figurative sense, however, the word has many possible translations: *puissant, émouvant, évocateur, vigoureux.*

> A cause du volume, sa voix était très puissante.
> *Because of its volume, his voice was most effective.*
>
> La scène du mariage était la plus émouvante.
> *The marriage scene was the most effective.*

26. End (of a month)

While "end of" is normally translated *la fin de* with months of the year the *de* is omitted, as is sometimes the article.

> La fin mars. . . .
> *The end of March. . . .*

27. Expect

"Expect" is best translated by the idiom *s'attendre à.*

> Je ne m'y attendais pas.
> *I didn't expect that.*

28. Fail

Note the difference in construction between *échouer* and *réussir*.

> Après beaucoup d'effort, il échoua.
> *After much effort, he failed.*
> Après beaucoup d'effort, il ne réussit pas à le convaincre.
> *After much effort he failed to convince him.*

29. Famous

"Famous" may be best rendered by *célèbre (bien) connu, renommé*.

> Un auteur bien connu (très renommé). . . .
> *A famous author.* . . .

Fameux is most often used in the sense of "great," "extraordinary," "legendary."

> Son impolitesse est fameuse.
> *His rudeness is famous.*   (*legendary*)

30. Feel

Note the various ways to render the English "feel."

> J'ai envie de danser.
> *I feel like dancing.*
> J'ai l'impression qu'il va changer d'avis.
> *I feel he may change his mind.*
> Je pense (je crois) qu'il a raison.
> *I feel he's right.*

31. Feelings

Be sure to distinguish between "feelings" (emotion)—*émotions*—and "feelings" (opinion)—*opinion* or *attitude*. The French word *sentiments*, like English "sentiments," however, can be used in both contexts.

32. Force (verb)

The phrase "to force upon" is never translated by *forcer*. Examine these

translations:

> Elle lui a imposé ses préjugés.
> Elle l'a contraint à accepter ses préjugés.
> *She forced her prejudices upon him.*

33. For example

"For example" is translated *par exemple* never *pour exemple*.

34. Future

The future is *l'avenir:*

> Il a un bel avenir.
> *He has a fine future.*

Le futur means the "future tense."
Note also "future" as an adjective is *futur(e)*:

> Sa vie future. . . .
> *His future life.* . . .

35. God

Never use the definite article with *Dieu* when capitalized. The article may be used only when the word refers to *a* god and, of course, is not capitalized.

> Les Romains appelaient le dieu de la guerre "Mars."
> *But:* Dieu a envoyé son fils sur terre.

(*Jésus Christ* is also used without an article; one says, however, *le Christ.*)

36. Hear from

The verb *entendre* can never be used in this phrase. Here are some translation possibilities:

> Ecris-moi un mot.
> Donnez-moi de vos nouvelles.
> *Let me hear from you.*

> Il nous a fait venir de ses nouvelles la semaine dernière.
> Nous avons reçu une lettre de lui la semaine dernière.
> *We heard from him last week.*

37. Ignore

Ignorer means "not to know":

> J'ignorais qu'il était malade.
> *I didn't know he was ill.*

"To ignore" is translated in various ways.

> Chaque fois qu'elle le voyait, elle refusait de le reconnaître.
> *She ignored him whenever she saw him.*

31

Elle ne tenait aucun compte de ses efforts de l'impressionner.
Elle feignait de ne pas voir ses efforts de l'impressionner.
She ignored completely his efforts to impress her.

38. Imagery

There is no separate French word for "imagery." The best translation is *les images*.

39. Introduce

"Introduce" is rendered by *introduire* in the sense of "to being in":

Qui a introduit le café en Europe?
Who introduced coffee in Europe?

When the verb means "to present people to one another," *présenter* must be used.

Il a oublié de nous présenter à l'hôte.
He forgot to introduce us to the host.

40. Just (adverb)

Note the variety of translations possible for this adverb:

Je viens de la voir.
I have just seen her.

Ses ennuis ne font que commencer.
Her troubles are just beginning.

C'est tout juste s'il est arrivé à payer ses dettes.
He just managed to pay his debts.

Je suis arrivé tout juste.
I arrived just in time.

41. Lecture

A "lecture" is *une conférence.*
Une lecture, means "a reading":

Une seule lecture du poème ne suffit pas pour comprendre la subtilité de son art.
A single reading of the poem does not suffice to understand the subtlety of its art.

32

42. Library

A "library" is *une bibliothèque. Une librairie* means "a bookstore."

43. Line

A "line" of verse—*un vers de poésie*
A "line" of prose—*une ligne de prose*

44. Live

"Live" as translated by *vivre* means essentially to be alive:

> Il vit!
> *He lives!*

The verb may be used, however, to indicate the act of residing in a place.

> J'y ai vécu longtemps.
> *I lived there for a long time.*

> On ne peut pas vivre à Paris.
> *You can't live in Paris.*

If you wish to be more specific and indicate residence in a house, on a particular street, etc., use *habiter* or *demeurer*.

> Il habite la troisième maison à gauche. (Il demeure dans la troisième maison à gauche.)
> *He lives in the third house on the left.*

Note that the expression "to live a life of" requires the verb "mener":

> Ils menaient une vie de. . . .
> *They lived a life of. . . .*

45. Maintain

"Maintain" is translated *maintenir* principally with *ordre* and *discipline*.

> Il ne pouvait pas maintenir l'ordre.
> *He could not maintain order.*

Where "maintain" really means "support" or "claim," the verb *soutenir* should be used.

> Il fallait l'effort de tout le monde pour soutenir la guerre.
> *Everyone's effort was needed to maintain the war.*

Where it means "to pursue," "keep up," use *entretenir*:

> Ils ne pouvaient pas entretenir une correspondance. . . .
> *They were not able to maintain a correspondence. . . .*

46. Make (with adjectives)

When the verb "make" is used with an adjective in the sense of "to render" the verb is best translated by *rendre* not *faire*.

Qu'est-ce qui rend ce personnage si intéressant?
What makes this character so interesting?

Note, however, this idiom: *se faire beau*—"to smarten up."

Je ne peux pas partir tout de suite, dit-elle, il me faut du temps pour me faire belle.
"I can't leave right away," she said, "I need some time to make myself presentable."

47. Marry

"To marry" is translated by *marier* in the following meanings only: perform the marriage ceremony (*Un évêque les maria*) and to marry one's child (*Il a marié sa fille*).

"To marry" meaning "to get married" is *se marier avec* or *épouser*.

Quoiqu'il fût riche, elle ne voulait pas l'épouser (se marier avec lui).
Despite his wealth, she did not want to marry him.

48. May (verb)

As the verb "may" can indicate both permission and possibility, and each meaning requires a different translation, you must distinguish the meaning before translating.

Sa mère dit qu'il peut venir.
His mother says he may come.   (permission)

Il se peut qu'il vienne, mais nous n'en sommes pas sûrs.
He may come but we're not sure.   (possibility)

49. Meet

"To meet" meaning "to run into" is translated by *rencontrer*.

Je l'ai rencontré devant l'opéra.
I met him in front of the opera.

"To meet" meaning "to make the acquaintance (of)" is *faire la connaissance (de)*.

Il attendait deux mois pour faire sa connaissance.
He waited two months to meet her.

50. Memory

Note these distinctions between *la mémoire* and *le souvenir*.
La mémoire means "memory" (the faculty to remember).

Après son accident, il a perdu la mémoire.
He lost his memory after the accident.

Le souvenir means "a memory" (a recollection).

Il a gardé un bon souvenir de ses vacances en France.
He kept a fond memory of his vacation in France.

51. Move

Note these possibilities of meaning and translation:
"to move" (emotionally)—*émouvoir*

Après son discours, nous étions très émus.
We were quite moved after his speech.

"to move" (physically)—*bouger*

Ne bougez pas; je veux prendre votre photo.
Don't move; I want to take your picture.

"to move away"—*déménager*

Nous serons obligés de déménager si mon père change de poste.
We'll be forced to move if my father changes jobs.

"to move into"—*aménager*

Ils venaient d'aménager, et ils n'avaient rien à manger.
They had just moved in, and they didn't have anything to eat.

52. Next

Note the particular translation of "next" in these phrases:

Nous avons manqué notre train. Voulez-vous attendre le suivant?
We missed the train. Do you want to wait for the next?

Je l'ai vu le lendemain.
I saw him the next day.

Je l'ai vu le lendemain matin.
I saw him the next morning.

Serez-vous chez vous mercredi prochain?
Will you be home next Wednesday?

Quand la prochaine réunion aura-t-elle lieu?
When will the next meeting take place?

53. Nothing

The pronoun *rien* followed by an infinitive requires *à* before the infinitive:

Il n'a rien à faire.
He has nothing to do.

Followed by an adjective, it requires *de* and the adjective is always masculine:

Qu'est-ce qu'il fabrique? Rien de bon.
What is he up to? Nothing good.

In sentences containing the phrase "never anything but," the word "anything" is best left untranslated:

> Elle ne parle que d'elle-même.
> *She never talks of anything but herself.*

54. Object (noun)

"Object" meaning "objective" is best translated by *but*.

> Il travaille sans but.
> *He works without any object.*

Note also these helpful phrases:

> A quoi visaient ses remarques?
> *What was the object of his remarks?*

> Il avait l'air de parler à la seule fin de nous ennuyer.
> *He seemed to speak with the single object of boring us.*

55. One (pronoun)

Never translate "the one" or "that one" by *l'un* or *l'une*. Use *celui* or *celle*:

> Je veux une cravate. Tu aimerais celle que j'ai vue ce matin.
> *I want a tie. You'd like the one I saw this morning.*

56. Oneself

If the word "himself," "herself," etc., is used as a direct object, in most cases you may not use the forms *lui-même, elle-même,* but a reflexive pronoun.

> Elle s'est tuée.
> *She killed herself.*

The forms with *-même* are used for other parts of speech, however.

> Il l'a fait lui-même.
> *He did it himself.*

> Il était fâché contre lui-même.
> *He was angry with himself.*

Note that there is a special form with *-même* for each person and one for each genre in the third person, *il—lui-même, elle—elle-même,* etc. *Soi-même* can only be used when the subject is *on*.

> Quand on est seul, on pense beaucoup à soi-même.
> *When one is alone, one thinks of oneself a great deal.*

57.   Opportunity

"Opportunity" is best translated by *occasion*. *Opportunité* does *not* exist.

> Nous avons rarement l'occasion de la voir.
> *We rarely have the opportunity to see her.*

58.   Outside

Both *dehors* and *en dehors de* mean "outside," but their use is quite different, as *dehors* is an adverb and *en dehors de* is a preposition. (*Hors de* is a synonym of *en dehors de.*)

> Qu'il attende dehors.
> *Let him wait outside.*   (adverb)

> Cela est en dehors de mon domaine.
> *That's outside my field.*   (preposition)

59.   Own (adjective)

"Own" is *propre*. Note, however, that in this sense the adjective is almost always placed before the noun it modifies.

> Ses propres idées. . . .
> *His own ideas. . . .*

Propre when it follows the noun usually changes meaning and is translated "clean" or "proper."

> Je cherche le sens propre du mot.
> *I'm looking for the proper meaning of the word.*

> Elle m'a apporté une chemise propre.
> *She brought me a clean shirt.*

60.   Paper (for a course)

"Paper" in this sense is translated *un devoir, une dissertation,* or simply *une composition.*

61.   Part

The words *la partie, le parti,* and *la part* are all quite separate in meaning and should not be confused.

La partie is "part" (of).

> Cette partie de la pièce est. . . .
> *This part of the play is. . . .*

Le parti means "party" (organization).

>Le Parti Communiste est. . . .
>*The Communist Party is.* . . .

Note also *prendre le parti de*—to make up one's mind to, *prendre parti pour (contre)*—to side with (against).

La part means "part" in the sense of "share."

>Je n'ai pas eu part dans l'affaire.
>*I had no part in the deal.*

Note also: prendre part à—take part in, pour ma part—as far as I'm concerned, d'une part . . . d'autre part—on the one hand . . . on the other hand.

62. Person

"Person" is normally translated *personne.*

>Je ne connais pas cette personne.
>*I don't know that person.*

When "person" is equivalent to "personage," *personnage* should be used and not *personne.*

>Il n'avait jamais fait la connaissance d'un personnage si éminent.
>*He had never met such an eminent person.*

63. Pity

"To pity" is *avoir pitié de. Pitier* does *not* exist.

>Elle n'eut pitié de personne.
>*She pitied no one.*

64. Place (noun)

Note these different possibilities for a translation of this word:

>La danse n'aura pas lieu.
>*The dance will not take place.*

>Ils ont trouvé un joli endroit où ils comptent passer l'été.
>*They found a nice place to spend the summer.*

>Etes-vous d'ici?
>*Are you from this place?*

>Quand nous sommes arrivés, il n'y avait pas de place pour nous.
>*When we arrived, there was no place for us.*

>Si j'étais à sa place. . . .
>*If I were in his place.* . . .

(Note that *la place* can also mean "square": cf. *La Place de la Concorde.*)

65. Plot

"The plot" of a play, a novel, etc., is *l'intrigue*. "Plot" meaning "conspiracy" is *le complot*.

66. Prejudiced

While the noun "prejudice" has its equivalent in *préjugé*, the adjective "prejudiced" must be translated by *prévenu* or *prédisposé* or some circumlocution.

Cf. Il a beaucoup de préjugés.
He is a very prejudiced man.

67. Rather

"Rather" meaning "slightly" is *assez* or *un peu*.

Il est assez (un peu) fou.
He is rather crazy.

"Rather" meaning "instead of" is *plutôt*.

Il court plutôt qu'il ne marche.
He runs rather than walks.

Plutôt is also used to express preference.

Il mourrait plutôt que de mendier.
He'd die rather than beg.

68. Reader

When using this word to refer to "the reader" of a book, etc., as contrasted with "the author," use *le lecteur*. The word *liseur* in French is actually an adjective meaning "fond of reading," and can be used as a noun only to mean "someone who reads a great deal."

C'est un grand liseur.
He's quite a reader.

69. Realistic

"Realistic" is translated *réaliste*.

"Unrealistic" or "unreal" must be rendered, however, by *irréel* (supernatural) or *invraisemblable* (improbable, unlikely).

70. Realize

While the verb *réaliser* is often used in modern French in the sense of "realize," its meaning is really "to bring into effect":

Il a réalisé ses rêves d'enfance.
He realized his childhood dreams.

"Realize" (to become aware of) is *se rendre compte de.*

Il s'est rendu compte qu'elle avait beaucoup de fautes.
He realized she had many faults.

71.   Recover

"Recover" meaning "to cover again" is *recouvrir.*

In its figurative meanings, however, you must choose from a large number of other verbs, depending on the nuance in the verb:

Il a retrouvé son écharpe.
He recovered (found) his scarf.

Il a repris ses sens. (Cf. also reprendre haleine, reprendre courage)
He recovered (got back) his reason.

Il s'est remis.   Il s'est rétabli.
He recovered from his illness.

72.   Remember

Do not confuse *se souvenir de* and *se rappeler,* which both mean "remember" but require different constructions.

Je m'en souviens.
Je me le rappelle.
I remember it.

Note because of the difference in structure only *se souvenir de* can be used with persons.

Je me souviens de lui.
I remember him.

73.   Rest (verb)

"To rest" is *se reposer:*

Repose-toi un instant.
Rest a while.

Rester mean "to remain."

Il est resté trois jours à Paris.
He stayed three days in Paris.

40

74.   Return

A correct translation of this verb depends on a precise awareness of its meaning.

"Return" meaning "to go back" is *retourner*.
"Return" meaning "to come back" is *revenir*.

> Il vient de revenir de Paris.
> *He has just returned from Paris (come back).*

> Compte-t-il y retourner?
> *Will he return (go back)?*

"Return" meaning "to go home" is *rentrer*.

> Il est tard, rentrons.
> *It's late, let's return (home).*

75. Sensitive

"Sensitive" is best translated by *sensible*, "sensitivity," by *sensibilité*.

> Sa poésie annonçait une âme bien sensible.
> *Her poetry revealed a very sensitive soul.*

"Sensible" meaning "having good sense" is *sensé, raisonnable*.

> Un homme sensé (de bon sens). . . .
> *A sensible man. . . .*

76. Significant

"Significant" may be translated in various ways: *important, significatif, de grande portée*, but *never* by *signifiant*, which is the present participle of *signifier*, only.

77. Something, some things

The expression *quelque chose* (something) has no plural form. "Some things" must be translated *des choses*.

> Il leur dit des choses d'une grande importance.
> *He told them some things of great import.*

78. Such

Both *tel* and *si* translate the English word "such," but their function is quite separate, as *tel* is an adjective and *si* is an adverb.

> Je n'achèterais jamais une telle chemise.
> *I'd never buy such a shirt.* (adjective)

> Il raconte des histoires si longues.
> *He tells such long stories.* (adverb)

Note also: "such" in an exclamation is *quel(le)*, etc.

> Quel bel enfant!
> *Such a beautiful child!*
> Quels beaux cheveux!
> *Such beautiful hair!*

79. Take (time)

"Take" with expressions of time is translated by *falloir*.

> Il faut deux heures de chemin de fer pour y arriver.
> *It takes two hours to get there by train.*

80. Take

Practice and study are necessary to translate this verb correctly. Examine carefully the following sentences:

> Prenez-le.
> *Take it. (Meaning "seize it.")*
> Menez-le chez le dentiste.
> *Take him to the dentist. (Meaning "lead him.")*
> Emmenez-le chez le dentiste.
> *Take him to the dentist. (Meaning "take him along.")*
> Emportez les chaises.
> *Take the chairs. (Meaning "take them away.")*
> Emmenez les femmes.
> *Take the women away.*

Note that "take away" is both *emporter* and *emmener* but that *emporter* is usually used with things and *emmener* with people. Do not confuse these verbs with *amener* and *apporter*, which mean "bring" and indicate movement toward the speaker or toward a place.

> Emmenez-le avec vous.
> *Take him with you. (Away from the speaker.)*
> Amenez-le avec vous.
> *Bring him with you. (Toward the speaker.)*

81. Tell

Do not confuse "tell"—*dire* (say)— and "tell"—*raconter* (tell a story).

> Il m'a dit non.
> *He told me no.*
> Il m'a tout raconté.
> *He told me all about it.*

82. That (the reason, the moment that)

While you are accustomed to translating "that" by *que* or *qui*, there are some expressions where "that" must be translated by other means:

> La raison pour laquelle. . . .
> *The reason that.* . . .
>
> Le moment où. . . .
> *The moment that.* . . .

83. Think of

"To think of" meaning "to think about" is *penser à*.

> Il est toujours en train de penser à elle.
> *He's always thinking of her.*

Penser de means "to have an opinion of."

> Que pensez-vous de ses poèmes?
> *What do you think of his poems?*

84. Time (at the same time)

Note the slight nuance in use among these translations:

> Elle pleurait et riait à la fois.
> *She was laughing and crying at the same time.*
>
> Il préparait un nouveau livre et en même temps il se demandait si cela valait la peine.
> *He was preparing a new book, and at the same time, he wondered if it were worthwhile.*
>
> Je l'admirais et cependant je le craignais.
> *I admired him and at the same time I feared him.*

85. Toward

"Toward" (a place) is translated *vers*.

> Il courut vers la forêt.
> *He ran toward the forest.*

Otherwise, in all figurative senses it is translated *envers*.

> Ils lui posèrent des questions sur l'attitude du général envers l'ONU.
> *They questioned him on the general's attitude toward the UN.*

86. Troubled

The adjective *troublé* most often means "troubled with emotion, stirred, thrilled."

43

Il ne la voyait jamais sans être troublé par elle.
He never saw her without being stirred by her.

"Troubled" meaning "disturbed," "upset" is best translated *inquiet, agité*.

Ils étaient très inquiets à cause de la mort du président.
They were greatly troubled by the death of the president.

87. Type

The noun *type* as used in colloquial modern French means "guy":

Qui est ce type-là?
Who's that guy?

Do not use it to translate "type" meaning "kind of."

Il a créé beaucoup de personnages de ce genre.
He has created many characters of this type.

Quelle sorte de conte aimez-vous lire?
What type of short story do you like to read?

88. Way (in this way)

"In" in this expression is never translated by *dans*, but by *de*.

De quelle façon devrais-je le faire?
In what way should I do this?

89. While

As the conjunction "while" may have several different connotations, it may have various translations.
"While" meaning "during" is *pendant que*.

Il est entré pendant que je parlais.
He came in while I was talking.

"While" meaning "whereas" is *tandis que*.

Il a opté pour la plage, tandis que moi, j'ai choisi une station d'hiver.
He chose the shore, while I picked a winter resort.

"While" meaning "although" is *bien que* or *quoique*.

Quoiqu'il pense avoir raison, il a tort.
While he thinks he's right, he's wrong.

44   90. Wise

"Wise" is best translated by *sage* in the sense of "prudent."

Il ne serait pas sage de faire cela.
It would not be wise to do that.

Otherwise, use *intelligent*.

> Il n'est pas aussi intelligent qu'il le pense.
> *He is not as wise as he thinks.*

NB *Sage* can also mean "well-behaved."

> Sois sage!
> *Be good!*

91.   Vis-à-vis

While this expression has retained in English the essence of its French meaning, do not forget that when using this expression in French, you must follow it with the preposition *de* or the appropriate contraction.

> Il nous a dit son attitude vis-à-vis du problème du Marché Commun.
> *He told us what his attitude was vis-à-vis the problem of the Common Market.*

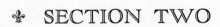 SECTION TWO

I Grammar Exercises

Ce and Il

1. Is this the easiest lesson in the book? —Yes, it is very simple.

—That's easy to say!

2. It is easy for him to know how to express himself because he is French.

—His mother was French. He is an American citizen. —But he learned

to speak French in France, not America.

3. I seem to have taken this scarf without knowing whose it was.

—That's hard to believe. You should have known it was mine.

—And that one there? Is that Mary's? —If it's the longest,

it must be hers.

4. He always insisted that *he* had understood the poem and

not the professor. —But he's the least sensitive (student) in the class!

I Grammar Exercises

CE AND IL

1. Is this the easiest lesson in the book? —Yes, it is very simple.
Est-ce la leçon la plus facile du livre? —Oui, elle[1] est très simple.

—That's easy to say!
—*C'est facile à dire!*

2. It is easy for him to know how to express himself because he is French.
Il lui est facile de savoir comment s'exprimer parce que c'est un Français.[2]

—His mother was French. He is an American citizen. —But he learned
—*Sa mère était Française. Il est citoyen américain. —Mais c'est*

to speak French in France, not America.
en France qu'il a appris à parler français et non pas aux Etats-Unis.[3]

3. I seem to have taken this scarf without knowing whose it was.
Il paraît que j'ai pris cette écharpe sans savoir à qui elle était.[4]

—That's hard to believe. You should have known it was mine.
—*C'est difficile à croire. Vous auriez dû[5] savoir qu'elle était à moi (la mienne).[6]*

—And that one there? Is that Mary's? —If it's the longest,
—*Et celle-là? Est-ce celle de Marie? —Si c'est la plus longue,*

it must be hers.
ce doit être la sienne.[7]

4. He always insisted that *he* had understood the poem and
Il insistait toujours que c'était lui qui avait compris le poème et

not the professor. —But he's the least sensitive (student) in the class!
non pas le professeur. —Mais c'est le moins sensible de la classe!

Y and En

1. Whenever the father called his son, he ran to him. The son rarely

disobeys him. I suppose he feels his father will never harm him.

He resembles him in everything and trusts him implicitly.

2. I could never get used to it. —To what? —To his passion for

insects. That's all he's interested in. —What does his wife think of

his spending his time dissecting insects? —She prefers not to think

of it at all. What he spends his time doing is of little interest to her.

3. I was going to visit her today, but I didn't feel

like it. Now I regret it. I had promised her too.

She had asked me to come in the past and asked me again.

I did not see her often and she was not happy at that. Nothing really

stopped me, and she would have been so grateful.

1. Whenever the father called his son, he ran to him. The son rarely
Quand le père appelait son fils, il courait à lui. Son fils lui désobéit

disobeys him. I suppose he feels his father will never harm him.
rarement. Je suppose[1] qu'il croit que son père ne lui nuira jamais.

He resembles him in everything and trusts him implicitly.
Il lui ressemble en tout et il se fie à lui complètement.

2. I could never get used to it. —To what? —To his passion for
Je ne pourrais jamais m'y habituer. —A quoi? —A sa passion pour

insects. That's all he's interested in. —What does his wife think of
les insectes. Il ne s'intéresse qu'à cela. —Que pense sa femme de[2]

his spending his time dissecting insects? —She prefers not to think
son habitude[3] de passer le temps à disséquer les insectes? —Elle préfère

of it at all. What he spends his time doing is of little interest to her.
ne pas y penser. Sa façon de passer le temps lui importe peu.

3. I was going to visit her today, but I didn't feel
J'avais l'intention de lui rendre visite[4] aujourd'hui, mais je n'en avais

like it. Now I regret it. I had promised her too.
pas envie. Maintenant, je le regrette. Je le[5] lui avais promis aussi.

She had asked me to come in the past and asked me again.
Elle m'avait demandé de venir dans le passé, et me l'avait redemandé.[6]

I did not see her often and she was not happy at that. Nothing really
Je ne la voyais pas souvent et elle n'en était pas contente. En vérité,

stopped me, and she would have been so grateful.
rien ne m'en empêchait, et elle en aurait été si reconnaissante.

Past Participle (Translate using passé composé)

1. When it began to rain, the guests got up and left

the garden. The chairs were brought in. As the hostess thought they

had been brought in too slowly, I took them all downstairs into the

basement to dry them off.

2. Because she had bought herself two new hats, she returned home

later than usual. As her husband was looking at the hats, which

he had found grotesque, she began to whine. —"I got them very

cheaply, and I've paid for them already. What will I do with them?"

—"Keep them, of course," her husband replied, "but I prefer the ones

you bought last year."

3. She remembered they had written one another once before. The letter

Past Participle (Translate using passé composé)

1. When it began to rain, the guests got up and left
Quand il a commencé à pleuvoir, les invités se sont levés et ont quitté

the garden. The chairs were brought in. As the hostess thought they
le jardin. On a rentré les chaises. Parce que l'hôtesse a pensé qu'on

had been brought in too slowly, I took them all downstairs into the
les avait rentrées trop lentement, je les ait toutes descendues dans le

basement to dry them off.
sous-sol pour les sécher.

2. Because she had bought herself two new hats, she returned home
Parce qu'elle s'était acheté deux chapeaux neufs,[1] elle est rentrée[2]

later than usual. As her husband was looking at the hats, which
plus tard que d'habitude. Pendant que son mari regardait les chapeaux

he had found grotesque, she began to whine. —"I got them very
qu'il avait trouvés grotesques, elle s'est mise à pleurnicher. —Je les ai

cheaply, and I've paid for them already. What will I do with them?"
eus à très bon marché,[3] et je les ai déjà payés.[4] Qu'est-ce que j'en

—"Keep them, of course," her husband replied, "but I prefer the ones
ferai? —Tu vas les garder, naturellement, a répondu le mari, mais je

you bought last year."
préfère ceux que tu as achetés l'année dernière.[5]

3. She remembered they had written one another once before. The letter
Elle s'est souvenu qu'ils s'étaient déjà écrit une fois. La lettre

53a

was in her old handbag. She took it out and reread it.

She realized then for the first time how much they thought

---

themselves in love with each other. They had never imagined

---

the end of the affair.

---

was in her old handbag. She took it out and reread it.
se trouvait dans son vieux sac. Elle l'a sortie[6] et elle l'a relue.

She realized then for the first time how much they thought
Alors pour la première fois elle s'est rendu compte combien ils s'étaient

themselves in love with each other. They had never imagined
crus amoureux l'un de l'autre.[7] Ils ne s'étaient jamais imaginé

the end of the affair.
la fin de l'affaire.

PARTITIVE

I'll take peaches, if you don't mind; I really don't like

plums. And as a rule (don't laugh), I never eat apples

because of the apples of my cousin's orchard. He no longer grows them

and hardly ever talks any more of the hours the family spent gathering

his fruits. Many times I have heard him say that most of the

apple trees died. But I know they were cut down. My grandfather

needed land. He felt one could do without apple trees

and needed a park. He dreamed of vast lawns and handsome statues

along the paths. I still remember little benches under

the oaks where my friends and I spent hours together as children.

Usually we spoke of unimportant things (we

PARTITIVE

I'll take peaches, if you don't mind; I really don't like
Je prendrai des pêches, s'il vous plaît; je n'aime pas beaucoup les

plums. And as a rule (don't laugh), I never eat apples
prunes. Et en général (ne riez pas), je ne mange jamais de pommes

because of the apples of my cousin's orchard. He no longer grows them
à cause des pommes du verger de mon cousin. Il ne les cultive plus

and hardly ever talks any more of the hours the family spent gathering
et ne parle guère plus des heures que la famille passait à cueillir

his fruits. Many times I have heard him say that most of the
ses fruits. Bien des fois je l'ai entendu dire[1] que la plupart des

apple trees died. But I know they were cut down. My grandfather
pommiers sont morts. Mais je sais qu'on les a abattus. Mon grand-père

needed land. He felt one could do without apple trees
avait besoin de terrain. Il croyait qu'on pouvait se passer de pommiers

and needed a park. He dreamed of vast lawns and handsome statues
et qu'on avait besoin d'un parc. Il rêvait de vastes pelouses et de belles

along the paths. I still remember little benches under
statues le long des allées. Je me souviens toujours de petits bancs sous

the oaks where my friends and I spent hours together as children.
les chênes où mes amis et moi passions[2] des heures ensemble quand nous

Usually we spoke of unimportant things (we
étions enfants. D'habitude nous parlions de choses peu importantes (nous

57a

never thought of the days to come), but sometimes we recalled

the apple trees, and confessed we missed them very much. Since

then I've never really felt like eating apples.

never thought of the days to come), but sometimes we recalled
ne pensions jamais aux jours à venir), mais quelquefois nous nous rappelions

the apple trees, and confessed we missed them very much. Since
les pommiers et nous avouions qu'ils nous manquaient[3] beaucoup. Depuis

then I've never really felt like eating apples.
lors je n'ai guère eu envie de[4] manger de pommes.

SUBJUNCTIVE

1. It's a shame you didn't discover this town before. There is

so much to see, provided you are willing to take long walks in

the broiling sun. Here, for example, is the first town hall

in France to be built after the war. I don't know of any

public building that is so unimpressive. I might point out

at the same time that should you wish to have a photograph of

that farmer and his horse, they will wait until you have

reloaded your camera. Of course, one must take care

the local inhabitants don't see you taking a picture of the old chateau.

It's the only building they care for. Personally, although I

have no strong feelings about this, I find it possible

SUBJUNCTIVE

1. It's a shame you didn't discover this town before. There is
C'est dommage que vous n'ayez pas découvert ce village auparavant. Il y a

so much to see, provided you are willing to take long walks in
tant à voir, pourvu qu'on veuille bien[1] faire de longues promenades par[2]

the broiling sun. Here, for example, is the first town hall
un soleil intense. Voici, par exemple, la première mairie qu'on

in France to be built after the war. I don't know of any
ait construite en France après la guerre. Je ne connais pas de

public building that is so unimpressive. I might point out
bâtiment public qui soit si peu impressionnant. Permettez-moi de

at the same time that should you wish to have a photograph of
vous indiquer en même temps que si vous voulez prendre une photo de

that farmer and his horse, they will wait until you have
ce fermier-là et de son cheval, ils attendront jusqu'à ce que vous

reloaded your camera. Of course, one must take care
ayez rechargé votre appareil. Bien entendu, il faut[3] prendre garde que

the local inhabitants don't see you taking a picture of the old chateau.
les gens du lieu ne vous voient photographier le vieux château.

It's the only building they care for. Personally, although I
C'est le seul bâtiment auquel ils tiennent. Quant à moi, quoique je

have no strong feelings about this, I find it possible
n'aie pas de sentiments prononcés à cet égard, je trouve qu'il est

61a

they may be quite right. Perhaps we should show respect

for what is worth being preserved.

2. It seems that her shares are no longer worth a great deal.

3. After the waves had washed away her footprints in the sand,

she felt a deep sadness.

4. He spoke to me very softly so that I didn't hear anything.

5. As far as I know, no one has knocked.

6. There was no lie she could tell to save him.

7. It seemed to me that people were always shaking hands in France.

8. If you call me and I'm not at home, try later.

9. Help us, if only for an instant.

10. "Let him die," the crowd cried out.

11. Tell the waiter to come and take our order.

they may be quite right. Perhaps we should show respect
possible qu'ils aient bien raison. Peut-être qu'on[4] devrait[3] montrer

for what is worth being preserved.
du respect pour ce qui mérite d'être préservé.

2. It seems that her shares are no longer worth a great deal.
Il semble que ses actions ne vaillent plus grand'chose.[5]

3. After the waves had washed away her footprints in the sand,
Après que les vagues eurent effacé ses pas sur le sable,

she felt a deep sadness.
elle ressentit une profonde tristesse.[6]

4. He spoke to me very softly so that I didn't hear anything.
Il m'a parlé très bas, de sorte que je n'ai rien entendu.[7]

5. As far as I know, no one has knocked.
Autant que je sache, personne n'a frappé.[8]

6. There was no lie she could tell to save him.
Il n'y avait pas de mensonge qu'elle pût prononcer pour le sauver.

7. It seemed to me that people were always shaking hands in France.
Il me semblait qu'on était toujours en train de se serrer la main en France.[9]

8. If you call me and I'm not at home, try later.
Si vous me téléphonez et que je ne sois pas chez moi, essayez plus tard.[10]

9. Help us, if only for an instant.
Aidez-nous, ne fût-ce qu'un instant.

10. "Let him die," the crowd cried out.
Qu'il meure, s'écria la foule.[11]

11. Tell the waiter to come and take our order.
Dites au garçon qu'il vienne prendre notre commande.[12]

63a

12. It is not clear that the crime was premeditated.

---

13. I doubt whether he would want to attend the debate.

---

14. It is hardly likely that's worth the effort.

---

15. Of those three girls, it's the prettiest (one) that I don't know.

---

16. "Wait until I think it over," he answered.

---

12. It is not clear that the crime was premeditated.
Il n'est pas clair que le crime fût prémédité.[13]

13. I doubt whether he would want to attend the debate.
Je doute s'il voudrait assister au débat.[14]

14. It is hardly likely that's worth the effort.
Il est peu probable que cela vaut la peine.[15]

15. Of those three girls, it's the prettiest (one) that I don't know.
De ces trois jeunes filles, c'est la plus jolie que je ne connais pas.[16]

16. "Wait until I think it over," he answered.
Attendez que je réfléchisse, répondit-il.[17]

Sequence of Tenses

(If two tenses, one for literary as well as conversational style, are possible, write both, putting the tense of literary style in parentheses.)

1. When you have a better sense of rhythm and rhyme, you

_____

can study Ronsard's lyricism.

_____

2. If I had such a comfortable apartment, I'd not want to move

_____

either.

_____

3. If they talk of romanticism, she talks of the decline of civilization.

_____

4. When the ministers had disapproved of the queen's behavior, they

_____

used to refuse her their counsel.

_____

5. Had you known him, you would have thought him eccentric.

_____

6. Before the dinner had begun, the guests knew the marriage was

_____

to be announced.

_____

Sequence of Tenses

(If two tenses, one for literary as well as conversational style, are possible, write both, putting the tense of literary style in parentheses.)

1. When you have a better sense of rhythm and rhyme, you
Quand vous aurez un sens de rythme et de rime plus développé, vous

can study Ronsard's lyricism.
pourrez étudier le lyrisme de Ronsard.

2. If I had such a comfortable apartment, I'd not want to move
Si j'avais un appartement si confortable, moi, non plus, je ne voudrais

either.
pas déménager.

3. If they talk of romanticism, she talks of the decline of civilization.
S'ils parlent du romantisme, elle parle du déclin de la civilisation.

4. When the ministers had disapproved of the queen's behavior, they
Quand les ministres[1] avaient désapprouvé le comportement de la reine, ils

used to refuse her their counsel.
lui refusaient leur conseil.

5. Had you known him, you would have thought him eccentric.
Si vous l'aviez connu,[2] vous l'auriez trouvé excentrique.

6. Before the dinner had begun, the guests knew the marriage was
Avant que le dîner ait (eût) commencé, les invités savaient qu'on allait

to be announced.
annoncer le mariage.

67a

7. As soon as the enemy had sighted the guards, they released

_____

the hostages.

_____

8. Napoleon wrote his memoirs while in exile.

_____

9. If they had waited until he finished, they would have appreciated

_____

his lecture more.

_____

10. It snowed during the night, and we did not know whether the

_____

roads were clear.

_____

7. As soon as the enemy had sighted the guards, they released
Aussitôt que l'ennemi a eu (eut) aperçu les gardes, ils ont libéré (libérèrent)

the hostages.
les otages.

8. Napoleon wrote his memoirs while in exile.
Napoléon a écrit (écrivit) ses mémoires pendant son exil.

9. If they had waited until he finished, they would have appreciated
S'ils avaient attendu qu'il ait (eût) terminé, ils auraient mieux

his lecture more.
apprécié la conférence.

10. It snowed during the night, and we did not know whether the
Il a neigé (neigea) pendant la nuit,[3] et nous ne savions pas si les

roads were clear.
routes étaient praticables.

Orthographic Changes

1. He takes his dog to the veterinarian every month.

___

2. She was arranging her papers when I called.

___

3. If he had to make a choice, he'd prefer to go with us.

___

4. Since he knows her well, bring her along too.

___

5. I'll be so happy when you throw that tie away.

___

6. He still pays her very little, although she cleans all the rooms

___

on this floor.

___

7. We were hoping you'd stay with us.

___

8. We weren't eating with him and he noticed.

___

9. We pronounce this word differently.

___

10. They get up very early in the morning.

___

ORTHOGRAPHIC CHANGES

1. He takes his dog to the veterinarian every month.
Il emmène son chien chez le vétérinaire tous les mois.

2. She was arranging her papers when I called.
Elle arrangeait ses papiers quand j'ai téléphoné.

3. If he had to make a choice, he'd prefer to go with us.
S'il lui fallait choisir, il préférerait aller avec nous.

4. Since he knows her well, bring her along too.
Puisqu'il la connaît bien, amenez-la aussi.

5. I'll be so happy when you throw that tie away.
Je serai si content quand vous jetterez[1] cette cravate.

6. He still pays her very little, although she cleans all the rooms
Il la paye[2] toujours très peu, bien qu'elle nettoie toutes les pièces[3]

on this floor.
à cet étage.

7. We were hoping you'd stay with us.
Nous espérions que vous descendriez[4] chez nous.

8. We weren't eating with him and he noticed.
Nous ne mangeions pas avec lui, et il s'en est aperçu.

9. We pronounce this word differently.
Nous prononçons ce mot différemment.[5]

10. They get up very early in the morning.
Ils se lèvent très tôt le matin.[6]

71a

II Translation Exercises

Exercise I

This play by Du Pont concerns the eternal struggle between

---

good and evil, the world of ideals and the world of lost souls.

He asks whether one who learns nothing from his present experience

---

can, in the future, achieve salvation. He introduces the reader

---

to two types of characters—those who enter the world of

---

everyday existence and those who live a life of regret after

---

having failed to find a place for themselves outside their

---

own universe, and it is through their interaction that the allegory

---

is made clear. While the author is actually a very sensitive writer,

---

it is rare that so famous a literary person

---

has used this technique. He may have selected this plot

II Translation Exercises

EXERCISE I

This play by Du Pont concerns the eternal struggle between
Dans cette pièce de Du Pont, il s'agit de(2) (18) la lutte éternelle entre

good and evil, the world of ideals and the world of lost souls.
le bien et le mal, le monde des idéaux[1] et celui(55) des âmes perdues.

He asks whether one who learns nothing from his present experience
Il demande si celui(55) qui ne profite point de[2] son expérience actuelle(3)

can, in the future, achieve salvation. He introduces the reader
peut, dans l'avenir(34) (39) obtenir(1) le salut. Il présente(39) au lecteur(68)

to two types of characters—those who enter the world of
deux sortes(87) de personnages(16)—ceux qui entrent dans le monde de

everyday existence and those who live a life of regret after
l'existence journalière et ceux qui mènent une vie(44) de regret après

having failed to find a place for themselves outside their
ne pas avoir réussi à(28) se trouver une place(64) en dehors de(58) leur

own universe, and it is through their interaction that the allegory
propre(59) univers, et c'est grâce au jeu[3] entre eux que l'allégorie

is made clear. While the author is actually a very sensitive writer,
s'éclaircit.[4] Bien que(89) l'auteur soit en vérité(3) un écrivain très

it is rare that so famous a literary person
sensible(75), il est rare qu'un personnage(62) littéraire si connu(29)

has used this technique. He may have selected this plot
ait employé cette technique. Il se peut(48) qu'il ait choisi cette intrigue(65)

73a

as part of his objective to show that a man who has never served

---

anyone but himself has no hope before God.

---

as part of his objective to show that a man who has never served
pour aider à son but (54) *de montrer*[5] *qu'un homme qui n'a jamais*

anyone but himself has no hope before God.
servi (53) *que lui-même ne peut plus espérer en Dieu* (35).

According to Du Pont, the hero finds it difficult to agree

_____

with his father, for he believes himself to be far wiser than

_____

his parent. The reason that the author raises this question

_____

has nothing to do with his feelings toward the boy; it is

_____

rather because he feels that his attitude is so characteristic

_____

of the sentiments of people of his age. At the same time, he shows

_____

how this individual, who during his youth had nothing

_____

to say to his father, may end by agreeing with him.

_____

It will all depend on whether he has understood that nothing good

_____

can come from such obstinacy. And Du Pont makes us wonder if there

_____

is in him the ability to see that the opportunity

_____

to learn what others have gotten from life should not be missed.

_____

According to Du Pont, the hero finds it difficult to agree
Selon Du Pont, le héros trouve qu'il est difficile de penser comme(6)

with his father, for he believes himself to be far wiser than
son père, car(10) *il se croit*(56) *infiniment*[1] *plus intelligent*(90) *que*

his parent. The reason that the author raises this question
son père. La raison pour laquelle(82) *l'auteur soulève cette question*

has nothing to do with his feelings toward the boy; it is
n'a rien à faire[2] *à ses sentiments*(31) *vis-à-vis du*(91) *garçon; c'est*

rather because he feels that his attitude is so characteristic
plutôt parce qu'il trouve que cette attitude est si caractéristique

of the sentiments of people of his age. At the same time, he shows
des opinions(31) *des gens*[3] *de son âge. En même temps*(84), *il montre*

how this individual, who during his youth had nothing
combien il se peut(48) *que cet individu, qui pendant sa jeunesse n'avait*

to say to his father, may end by agreeing with him.
rien à(53) *dire à son père, finisse par tomber*[4] *d'accord*(6) *avec lui.*

It will all depend on whether he has understood that nothing good
Tout dépendra de sa compréhension du fait qu'un tel(78) *entêtement ne*

can come from such obstinacy. And Du Pont makes us wonder if there
peut rien produire de(53) *bon. Et Du Pont nous fait nous demander s'il*

is in him the ability to see that the opportunity
a la capacité de voir qu'on ne devrait[5] *pas manquer l'occasion*(57)

to learn what others have gotten from life should not be missed.
d'apprendre ce que d'autres ont tiré de la vie.

It is true that certain critics, noting this letter,

_____

have gone so far as to maintain that only afterward did Stendhal

_____

become aware of the resemblances which existed between Mary and

_____

Mathilde's personalities and only to explain to some friends to

_____

what degree his own creation was plausible. This

_____

interpretation is unacceptable. We must believe what Stendhal himself

_____

has told us: Mary was for him . . . a stimulus, which encouraged him to

_____

rework a personality he had already sketched. . . . Meanwhile, Stendhal . . .

_____

was about to encounter new loves. At the end of January a

_____

pretty young Italian girl . . . was making the most unexpected advances to him; soon

_____

she was giving herself to him and making him ask for her hand in marriage.

_____

It is true that certain critics, noting this letter,
Il est vrai que certains critiques(20), en faisant état de cette lettre,

have gone so far as to maintain that only afterward did Stendhal
sont allés jusqu'à vouloir[1] soutenir(45) que Stendhal ne s'est aperçu

become aware of the resemblances which existed between Mary and
qu'après coup des ressemblances qui existaient entre les caractères(16)

Mathilde's personalities and only to explain to some friends to
de Mary et de Mathilde et seulement pour expliquer à quelques amis jusqu'à

what degree his own creation was plausible. This
quel point(24) sa propre(59) création était vraisemblable(69). Cette

interpretation is unacceptable. We must believe what Stendhal himself
interprétation est inadmissible. Il faut croire ce que Stendhal lui-même

has told us: Mary was for him . . . a stimulus, which encouraged him to
nous a dit: Mary a été pour lui . . .[2] un stimulant qui l'encouragea à

rework a personality he had already sketched. . . . Meanwhile, Stendhal . . .
remanier un caractère qu'il avait déjà esquissé. . . . Sur ces entrefaites

was about to encounter new loves. At the end of January a
Stendhal allait . . . connaître de nouvelles amours.[3] Fin janvier(26) une

pretty young Italian girl . . . was making the most unexpected advances to him; soon
jeune et jolie Italienne . . .[4] lui faisait les avances les plus imprévues; bientôt

she was giving herself to him and making him ask for her hand in marriage.
elle se donnait à lui et se faisait demander en mariage.[6]

Exercise IV

His . . . originality, then, consists in developing the tiniest anecdote,

in making plausible the most outlandish news item. There lies

the triumph of his reason, of his intuitive knowledge of what motivates

the human mind, of the ins and outs of the disturbed conscience.

Accumulating small touches, short explanations, successive and rapid

notations, through his sheer force of deduction, which is exerted

on what he has constructed by instinct, he succeeds in making seemingly

insane actions look rational and the most gratuitous turns of fate

look necessary. Thus, almost always he gets his start by observing life,

as he needs elegant events and illustrious examples if the efforts

of his creative genius are to achieve full results.

His . . . originality, then, consists in developing the tiniest anecdote,
Son originalité . . . consiste alors à développer la plus mince anecdote,

in making plausible the most outlandish news item. There lies
à rendre(46) plausible le fait divers le plus exceptionnel. C'est là le

the triumph of his reason, of his intuitive knowledge of what motivates
triomphe de sa raison, de sa connaissance intuitive des ressorts[1] de

the human mind, of the ins and outs of the disturbed conscience.
l'esprit humain, des détours de la conscience troublée(86).

Accumulating small touches, short explanations, successive and rapid
Accumulant les petites touches, les explications menues, les notations

notations, through his sheer force of deduction, which is exerted
successives et pressées, par sa seule force de déduction s'exerçant

on what he has constructed by instinct, he succeeds in making seemingly
sur ce qu'il a construit d'instinct, il arrive à rendre(46) raisonnables

insane actions look rational and the most gratuitous turns of fate
des actions folles en apparence, nécessaires les péripéties les plus

look necessary. Thus, almost always he gets his start by observing life,
gratuites. Il part ainsi presque toujours de l'observation du réel,

as he needs elegant events and illustrious examples if the efforts
car(10) il a besoin de beaux cas et d'exemples illustres pour que son

of his creative genius are to achieve full results.
génie créateur puisse s'employer avec un plein rendement.

[A critic compares Freud's theory of aggressive laughter (deriving pleasure from ridiculing our enemy) with Baudelaire's satanic laugh.]

Comedy and poetry use analogous methods to arrive at

_____

opposite results. It would seem, then, that Freud's tendentious laugh,

_____

which is almost the same as Baudelaire's satanic laugh,

_____

is the most removed from the world of poetry. There exists in poetry,

_____

nevertheless, a . . . region where these two opposites come together:

_____

the region of irony, which is always aggressive and destructive like the

_____

tendentious laugh itself. Baudelaire's irony, however, has a

_____

completely different function from tendentious comedy, for instead of

_____

representing an aggression on the part of the id and the "self," it depends

_____

almost entirely on the creative self, on the world of poetry. That is

_____

true for La Lune Offensée and Le Coucher du Soleil Romantique where

_____

Comedy and poetry use analogous methods to arrive at
La comédie et la poésie usent de[1] *moyens analogues afin d'obtenir des*[1]

opposite results. It would seem, then, that Freud's tendentious laugh,
résultats contraires. Il semblerait donc que le rire tendancieux de

which is almost the same as Baudelaire's satanic laugh,
Freud—qui correspond à peu près au rire satanique de Baudelaire—

is the most removed from the world of poetry. There exists in poetry,
soit le plus opposé à l'ordre poétique. Il existe pourtant en poésie

nevertheless, a . . . region where these two opposites come together:
une région . . . où ces deux contraires se rencontrent:

the region of irony, which is always aggressive and destructive like the
celle[2] *de l'ironie, toujours agressive et destructrice, comme le*

tendentious laugh itself. Baudelaire's irony, however, has a
rire tendancieux lui-même. L'ironie baudelairienne[3] *a cependant une*

completely different function from tendentious comedy, for instead of
toute autre fonction que le comique[4] *tendancieux, car, au lieu de*

representing an aggression on the part of the id and the "self," it depends
représenter une agression de[5] *la part du id et du "moi," elle dépend*

almost entirely on the creative self, on the world of poetry. That is
presque entièrement du "moi" créateur, de l'ordre poétique. Cela est

true for La Lune Offensée and Le Coucher du Soleil Romantique where
vrai pour La Lune Offensée et Le Coucher du Soleil Romantique où

Baudelaire extols his own esthetic at the same time he attacks the vulgarity

of the century, and even for A Une Madone, where the poet, while

fiercely attacking his mistress, also assails his own "self"

as these two beings seem inferior to the true Madonna and

Creator. The best example of this fierce irony, which is close to the

satanic laugh, comes in l'Héautotontimorouménos where the creative "self"

scores a definitive victory over the other. Thus does Baudelaire's

irony place the tendentious laugh at the service of the poetic world which

succeeds through it in destroying the "self" and the id where it usually

finds its source. Here we have a veritable reversal of role and

function, for the satanic laugh, far from affirming the superiority of the

individual, carries it away into nothingness, allowing only

the poetic effect to remain.

Baudelaire extols his own esthetic at the same time he attacks the vulgarity
Baudelaire prône sa propre esthétique tout en[6] s'attaquant à la vulgarité

of the century, and even for A Une Madone, where the poet, while
du siècle, et même pour A Une Madone, où le poète, tout en

fiercely attacking his mistress, also assails his own "self"
s'attaquant férocement à sa maîtresse, s'en prend également à son propre

as these two beings seem inferior to the true Madonna and
"moi": ces deux êtres apparaissent comme inférieurs à la vraie Madone et

Creator. The best example of this fierce irony, which is close to the
au Créateur. Le meilleur exemple de cette ironie féroce, voisine du rire

satanic laugh, comes in l'Héautotontimorouménos where the creative "self"
satanique, se trouve dans l'Héautotontimorouménos où le "moi"

scores a definitive victory over the other. Thus does Baudelaire's
créateur l'emporte définitivement sur l'autre. L'ironie baudelairienne

irony place the tendentious laugh at the service of the poetic world which
met ainsi le rire tendancieux au service de l'ordre poétique qui

succeeds through it in destroying the "self" and the id where it usually
parvient grâce à lui à détruire le "moi" et le id où il trouve

finds its source. Here we have a veritable reversal of role and
d'habitude sa source. On a là un véritable renversement de rôle et de

function, for the satanic laugh, far from affirming the superiority of the
fonction, car le rire satanique, loin d'affirmer la supériorité de

individual, carries it away into nothingness, allowing only
l'individu, l'entraîne avec lui dans le néant, ne laissant subsister

the poetic effect to remain.
que l'effet poétique.

 APPENDICES

Appendix I

Ce and Il

[1] Note that while *ce* may have many uses and translations—"that," "this," "it"—with an adjective alone (not followed by a dependent infinitive) it can be used to translate "that" only: *C'est très facile.* (*That* is very easy.) If the pronoun "it" occurs, you must use *il* or *elle*, depending on the antecedent.

[2] In French, adjectives indicating nationality are capitalized when they mean a person of that nationality—*un Français* means "a Frenchman." Otherwise these adjectives as well as names of languages are *not* capitalized in French.

[3] Do not use *Amérique* to translate "America" when you mean the United States. *Amérique* in French has a broad meaning and is more the equivalent of "North America."

[4] For the use of the pronoun, see note 1.

[5] Do not be confused by the defective verbs "should" and "ought" in English which have no perfect forms. The verb *devoir* is not defective, so that "ought to have," "should have" in French are a simple present perfect form.

[6] Note this synonym form for *à moi*. The pronoun exists for each person, *le tien, le sien, le nôtre, le vôtre, le leur,* singular and plural, *les tiens,* etc., masculine and feminine *la sienne, la vôtre,* etc.

89

⁷ Note here now *ce* keeps its demonstrative value. "It" here (vs. the pronoun discussed in note 1) is used to describe an object at some distance from the speaker. "It" here means in essence "that one"; and *ce*, not *elle*, is used.

Y and En

¹ Note that *supposer* requires the subjunctive only when expressing a clear case of hypothesis.

> Supposons qu'il ait fait cela. . . .
> *Let us suppose he did that. . . .*

² Distinguish carefully between *penser de*, which means "think of" (have an opinion), and *penser à*, which is "think of" (be thinking of).

³ A noun has to be inserted here as French does not possess this verbal noun construction.

⁴ To "visit" a person is *rendre visite à*. *Visiter* is used for cities and countries.

⁵ Note that while the pronoun may not be expressed in English, it must always be present in French.

⁶ The prefix *re-*, meaning "again," is very common in French. Watch for other forms in your reading.

Past Participle

¹ "New" is translated by *neuf* to indicate what is brand-new. "*Nouveau*" is used for what is newly acquired, different, or newly created.

² See Reference Dictionary #74.

³ Note that the adjective *bon marché* becomes an adverb by the addition of the preposition *à*. As adjective it is invariable:

> *Des articles bon marché. . . .*

The comparative form is *meilleur marché* (*à meilleur marché* for the adverb).

⁴ There is no preposition with the verb *payer*. *Payer* means "to pay for" (something). *Payer pour* means to "pay for" (someone).

> Je paye pour nous tous.
> *I'm paying for all of us.*

⁵ "Last year" is *l'année dernière*. *La dernière année* means "the last year" (of a series). Compare the following sentences:

> *J'ai vu cela la semaine dernière.*
> *C'est la dernière semaine du mois.*

⁶ "To take" (something from its place) can also be expressed by the verb *prendre* in which case the preposition used indicates where the object was *prior* to its removal:

> Elle l'a prise dans son sac.
> *She took it out of her bag.*

> Il a pris le livre sur le rayon.
> *He took the book from the shelf.*

90

⁷ As reflexive constructions indicate an action done to the self, an expression such as *l'un, l'autre* is necessary to transform a reflexive meaning into one of reciprocity. *Ils s'étaient crus amoureux* means only "They had thought themselves in love." It is the addition of *l'un, l'autre* that changes the meaning to

"in love with each other." The preposition used between *l'un, l'autre* is determined by the adjective or verb involved. Cf. *amoureux de* but: *Ils s'étaient écrit l'un à l'autre.* (*écrire à*)

PARTITIVE

[1] Many common verbs like *vouloir, sembler,* and *entendre* require no preposition before the dependent infinitive.

[2] In the case of a compound subject the person of the verb is determined thusly: where the subject contains a pronoun of the first person, the verb is in the first person; a pronoun of the second person but none of the first person, the verb is in the second person; if pronouns of the third person only, the verb is in the third person.

[3] While modern usage is not consistent in this regard, the verb *manquer* is best used in the impersonal construction with the person indicated by an indirect object pronoun and the item expressed by the subject or the partitive:

> Il me manque du papier. (Le papier me manque.)
> *I lack paper.*

Note also that the same construction is used when the verb means "miss":

> Elle me manque.
> *I miss her.*

[4] Note the idiom *avoir envie de,* "to feel like."

SUBJUNCTIVE

[1] *Vouloir* means "to want." *Vouloir bien* means "to be willing."

[2] Note this use of *par* to translate "in" with elements of weather.

> Cf. Vous n'allez pas sortir par un tel temps!
> *You're not going out in such weather!*

[3] An important and not that subtle distinction exists between *falloir* and *devoir* which is not always apparent from the English verb to be translated. *Falloir* is used in cases where one acts out of necessity; *devoir* is used in cases of social and moral obligation.

[4] Note the insertion of *que* after *peut-être*. When *peut-être* begins a sentence in conversational style, this *que* is used to avoid inversion of verb and subject which *must* appear in literary style, e.g., *Peut-être devrait-on.* . . . This inversion in literary style is also used with *sans doute* and *aussi* (when *aussi* means "therefore").

[5] *Il semble* takes the subjunctive. The same sentence with *Il paraît,* however, would require the indicative.

[6] Note that though *avant que* requires the subjunctive, *après que* always is followed by the indicative. For the verb form see Sequence of Tenses, III, 3.

[7] When *de sorte que* indicates result rather than purpose, the indicative is required. Cf.:

91

> Il m'a parlé très bas de sorte que personne ne pût nous entendre.
> *He spoke to me very softly so that no one might hear us.*

[8] Note this particular use of the present subjunctive of *savoir.* The phrase is a fixed expression as is *pas que je sache* (not that I know, not to my knowledge).

⁹ Be sure not to confuse *il semble,* which requires the subjunctive, with "it seems to me, to us," etc. (*il me semble*), which requires the indicative.

¹⁰ The *que* which replaces *si* in a series of subordinate clauses is considered a contraction of *à condition que,* an expression used with the subjunctive.

¹¹ An important, though not frequent, use of the subjunctive is to express an imperative in the third person. Do not confuse this imperative "let" with the "let" of permission, which is translated by *laisser* or *permettre.*

¹² This is a variant on the imperative subjunctive. When verbs like *dire* or *faire savoir* have the force of giving a command, the verb which indicates what was said (ordered) is in the subjunctive.

¹³ While certain impersonal expressions like *il est vrai, il est clair,* take the indicative, put into a negative or interrogative form, they are usually followed by the subjunctive.

¹⁴ *Douter que* ("to doubt that") takes the subjunctive, but *douter si* ("to doubt whether") takes the indicative.

¹⁵ Another annoying pair is *il est probable,* which requires the subjunctive, and *il est peu probable,* which seems so nearly definite a statement that the indicative is used.

¹⁶ Notice the difference between this construction and *C'est la jeune fille la plus jolie que je connaisse,* and the different mode used with each.

¹⁷ In spoken French it is common to contract *attendre jusqu'à ce que* to *attendre que,* but the subjunctive is still used.

Sequence of Tenses

¹ Do not confuse *le ministre* (minister) with *le ministère* (ministry).

² Note the variety of constructions possible in English, but French has only one.

³ Note the use of the past (in)definite here and not the imperfect, though we are dealing with duration. The imperfect may not be used because the clause indicates both the beginning and the completion of the action:

> Cf. Il parlait quand je suis entré.
> *He was talking when I came in.*

We do not know when he stopped talking, and because the sentence presents an action in progress, continuing in the past, the imperfect (*parlait*) is used. In *il a neigé pendant la nuit* (it snowed during the night), there is no such description of a continuing action, but merely the declaration that an action took place and was completed in the past.

Orthographic Changes

¹ *Jeter* is not only "to throw" but "to throw away."

² Verbs ending in *ayer* may keep the *y* before the mute *e.*

³ "Room" in general sense is translated by *pièce. Chambre* means "bedroom," *salle,* a large room or a special room when modified as in *salle à manger* (dining room).

⁴ When "stay" means "to stay" (at a hotel, with friends, etc.), it must be translated by *descendre,* not *rester.*

[5] All adjectives ending in *-ent* or *-ant* end in *-e(a)mment* in their adverbial form.

[6] "In" with parts of the day is usually not translated.

Cf. J'aimais lire l'après-midi (le soir).
I liked to read in the afternoon (evening).

Appendix II

Exercise I

[1] Note this irregular plural for nouns (and masculine adjectives) ending in *-al*. Cf. *cheval, chevaux, social, sociaux,* etc. *Idéals* is acceptable, however.

[2] Note that "to learn from" (benefit from) is best translated by a verb other than *apprendre*.

[3] There is no French word which is as explicit as "interaction." *Jeu* is a good translation when "interaction" = "interplay."

[4] Note how French avoids the English passive through the reflexive verb. This is a definite characteristic of French style and should be imitated whenever possible.

[5] Do not confuse *montrer*, which means "to show" (point out) and *démontrer*, which means "to show" in the sense of "demonstrate" (establish the truth of).

Exercise II

[1] Note that adjectives which end in a vowel do *not* use the feminine form of the adjective to form the adverb, e.g., *poli—poliment, joli—joliment.*

² Do not confuse *avoir à faire* [to have (something) to do]—*Il n'a rien à faire.* (He has nothing to do.)—with *avoir affaire à* [to have something to do (with someone)]:

> Je ne veux plus avoir affaire à eux.
> *I don't want to have anything more to do with them.*

> Attention, vous aurez affaire à moi!
> *Be careful, (or) you'll have to deal with me!*

³ Note that French makes a rather strict distinction between "people"—the collective noun denoting a geographic, political group:

> the people of Paris—le peuple de Paris
> government by the people—le gouvernement du peuple

and the collective noun indicating a social group, or simply a small group:

> you young people—vous autres jeunes gens
> many people—beaucoup de gens
> They are nice people.—Ce sont de braves gens.

⁴ Did you follow the normal tendency to use the present participle in French? The present participle in French is above all an adjective, not a noun. The noun equivalent in French is usually the infinitive:

> Voir c'est croire.
> *Seeing is believing.*

But:

> Ils s'en allèrent, chantant à tue-tête.
> *They went away, singing loudly.*

The present participle in French, like the passive voice, should be used sparingly. When introduced in English by a preposition ("for," "to," etc.), the French uses the infinitive (only *en* may be followed in French by the present participle); when introduced in English by a verb, it will likewise most regularly be translated by an infinitive, especially if the verb requires a preposition:

> Entendre chanter. . . . *Hear singing.* . . .
> Aimer aller. . . . *Like going.* . . .

> succeed in finding—réussir à trouver
> finish by saying—finir par dire

⁵ See Appendix I, Subjunctive, note 3.

EXERCISE III

¹ Note that a number of very common verbs in French do *not* require a preposition before the dependent infinitive:

vouloir dire	savoir conduire
préférer mourir	aimer chanter
aller danser	entendre pleurer

² The author is obviously paraphrasing here. Were he quoting Stendhal's actual words, he would have been obliged to alter the original text, as you cannot move from third to first person within the same sentence. Stendhal's statement is doubtlessly in the first person and might have been worded: *"J'ai trouvé chez Mary un stimulant. . . ."* It would have been impossible for the author to write, *"Stendhal nous dit que 'j'ait trouvé'. . . ."* (Stendhal tells us that I find. . . .) as logic insists on use of the third person throughout (Stendhal tells us that *he* finds. . . .). If you do not choose to paraphrase your text and wish to quote exactly, you must alter the text so that it forms

a coherent whole and place each change within brackets, e.g., *Stendhal nous dit qu'* "[il] [a] trouvé. . . ."

³ Note that some nouns in French, e.g., *amour, orgue,* and *délice,* are masculine in the singular but feminine in the plural.

⁴ Note how a nice economy of words is achieved in French by using adjectives denoting nationality as nouns.

⁵ Study carefully this construction with *faire.* It is known as the "causative *faire*" and is used to indicate an action which (with a reflexive pronoun) literally "is made to be done" (though the French uses the active not the passive infinitive:

> Elle s'est fait faire une robe.
> *She had a dress made.*

(Notice also how the reflexive pronoun is often left untranslated.) When *faire* is not reflexive, the expression means "to have someone do something":

> Elle l'a fait danser.
> *She made him dance.*

EXERCISE IV

¹ Each of the words italicized in this passage is particularly important through its frequency in modern French and its diversity in meaning. They should be studied carefully and their various meanings learned.

ressort—literally "spring," it can also mean in a figurative sense, "incentive," "impetus," "motivation."

esprit—"spirit" (le Saint Esprit); "wit" (Il a de l'esprit.); "mind" (Il a perdu l'esprit.); "dominant feeling" (L'esprit public était contre.).

détour—literally "turn" (in a road), it may be any circuitous way or winding (in speech, geography or thought).

s'exercer—literally "to drill," "do exercises," but with "sur" it means "exert upon"; with "dans," "hold sway": Ses idées s'exercent toujours dans la biologie moderne.

péripétie—literally, "a sudden turn of events in a plot," but in the plural the word may mean simply "vicissitudes," "adventures."

gratuit—literally "free" (of charge), also means "gratuitous," (unwarranted).

s'employer—The verb may mean "exert oneself," "spend one's time," "interest oneself in" (with preposition *pour*).

rendement—literally "yield," this word can indicate the produce of the ground, output of a factory, the result of any effort. Note: *travailler à plein rendement* (to work full time).

EXERCISE V

¹ Note this example of differences in use of the partitive with plural nouns. The *des* follows the general rule but the *de* must be used in the first instance because of the expression *user de*. Cf. Partitive, p. 9, Other Pecularities 2.

² Appreciate the use of this pronoun, very normal in French, in a case where a literal translation (that of irony) would not be desirable in English.

³ Adjectives formed from authors' names are very common in French and widely used in critical writing. Cf. *gidien, sartrien, shakespearien, moliéresque, rimbaldien, hugolien, racinien,* etc.

⁴ Note the use of *le comique* in contexts where English is more likely to use the word "comedy." *La comédie* in French means essentially "a funny play"; in a figurative sense, "a funny situation." *Le comique* means literally "the comic element."

Cf. La situation est passée de la tragédie à la comédie.
The situation went from (one of) tragedy to comedy.

Mais son mari a refusé d'y voir tout ce qu'il y avait de comique.
But her husband refused to see any of the comedy in it.

⁵ Note "on" in "on the part of" is translated by *de*.

⁶ *Tout en* meaning literally "even while" is a very useful expression and is always followed by the present participle.

Supplementary Exercises

I. Grammar Material

Gender (Translate)

1. The poet obviously gave much attention to the composition of his poem.
2. He is in a good humor today.
3. Romanticism and Classicism are often opposed as being two distinct literary schools.
4. There was little movement in the play's last act.
5. There is a person I can't stand!

Ce and Il (Translate)

1. Tell him to come immediately. It's important.
2. It is important that he come on time.
3. He is important to the national security.
4. Is that my glove lying on the table?
5. No, it's lying on the chair.

Y and *En* (Replace the following nouns or phrases introduced by "à" or "de" by the appropriate pronoun.)

1. Il voulait acheter des timbres.
2. Il ne songeait plus à son désir de lui mentir.
3. Elle m'avait demandé plusieurs fois de vous téléphoner.
4. Le roi François I succéda à son beau-père.
5. La situation ressemblait beaucoup à la crise de 1929.

Agreement of the Past Participle (Translate)

1. I bought some yesterday.
2. The song she learned by heart was very amusing.
3. She died very young.
4. They (F.) wrote one another every day.
5. She complained very little about her marks.

Partitive (Translate)

1. He likes beer very much.
2. He eats a great deal of bread every meal.
3. Most of the time there are not enough hours in the day.
4. Most of the classroom was dark.
5. She no longer needs the books you loaned her.

Subjunctive (Translate)

1. I think you may be wrong.
2. He hopes it will not rain tomorrow.
3. He fears it will rain tomorrow.
4. I'm surprised you don't know that.
5. Be careful your brother doesn't lose his money.

Sequence of Tenses (Translate)

1. Whenever she speaks, he leaves the room.
2. When he finishes, tell him to show me his work.
3. Were I to go, would you stay?
4. He wanted us to have dinner with him.
5. When the snow had melted, she would look for the first flowers of spring.

Orthographic Differences (Translate)

1. I've lost the committee's address.
2. His manner and language were aggressive.
3. The enemy was responsible for the appearance of a new dictator.

4. History repeatedly shows the desire of every civilization to develop its own character.
5. He wrote of exaggerated enthusiasm and exaggerated melancholy.

Orthographic Changes (Translate)

1. The concert was beginning and we were still eating.
2. Clean your room carefully!
3. Would you buy such a large house?
4. I'll wash the dishes but I'll not wipe them.
5. I'd call him "Jean" if I were you.

II. TRANSLATION MATERIAL

I.

1. She entered the room without my noticing.
2. He promised to do it, but actually I never thought he would.
3. What a reader! You've always a book in your hand.
4. She was always too sensitive to be sensible.
5. Mother says I may go, but I may arrive late.

II.

1. Old people should be treated with respect.
2. Your attitude is at the same time tragic and laughable.
3. In the Middle Ages kings did little for the people.
4. Such a beautiful dress, and on such a beautiful girl!
5. What have you gotten from reading Mann?

III.

1. He bored us to such a degree that we left.
2. What you are doing is not quite proper.
3. What do you think of modern literary criticism?
4. Remorse came to him only afterward.
5. He maintained that his cause was just.

IV.

1. She always buys such fine furs.
2. We live in a very troubled world.
3. You make every problem seem so simple.
4. He always reacts instinctively.
5. He takes as his point of departure the fact that his students want to learn.

V.

1. We can decide now where to meet after the game.
2. The critics assailed his lack of form.
3. Their handwritings are not at all alike.
4. That depends on your knowledge of your subject.
5. The proper meaning of this word is very close to its German equivalent.

III. MATERIAL APPENDED TO GRAMMAR EXERCISES

1. It is always difficult to know what you think of the books you read.
2. Every summer we visit friends in Paris.
3. These dresses are sold more cheaply in America.
4. The last week she was in Europe, she missed her family very much.
5. Is her father willing to let you come? —Not that I know.
6. The authorities told him he was never to return to the village again.
7. 8. She asked me if it was snowing when the accident occurred. —It snowed all night, I answered, but the snow had stopped by dawn.
9. She is waiting patiently for him to throw away his old shirts.
10. I have decided how long to stay, but not where to stay.

IV. REFERENCE DICTIONARY

The success of Molière's humor depends largely on his ability to make his characters vivid and human even while making them seem ridiculous. For this reason, we remember his characters so easily, and if, on the other hand, their names escape us, their personalities are unforgettable.

His plays are often concerned with that type of character who spends his time cultivating an image of himself that is false—Monsieur de Pourceaugnac, for example, who does not want to be taken for a provincial and affects city manners.

It does not take long for his plot to commence. Directly or indirectly, he usually presents his main character in the first scene and constructs the action around the character's relation to the other actors.

Molière knew his audience well. To create his characters he must certainly have put himself in their place, thinking at the same time of the audience and their reactions. When Monsieur de Pourceaugnac fears he will be hanged and changes clothes to disguise himself, Molière is telling us something about the character of this "hero." But he is also preparing the laughter of the audience before such a sight.

Because so much of Molière's comedy is visual, it is difficult to appreciate all of his humor upon reading the plays; but any sensitive reader who is capable of visualizing the action will soon realize the genius of this author.

101

V. MATERIAL APPENDED TO THE TRANSLATION EXERCISES

1. Show me how to profit best from such exercises.
2. Every politician has to deal politely with the people.

3. She knew he didn't like to dance, although he learned to dance when very young.

4. 5. Most exercises of this type are done too quickly. Students don't like taking the time required to think about the grammatical constructions in question.

6. The social and cultural aspects of this phenomenon show how worthy it is of new study.

7. Who knows what was the incentive behind such an action?

8. When he returned from Europe, he spoke of his diverse loves, a young French girl, two English girls, and a Swedish girl.

9. They are having a house built instead of buying one.

10. He was constantly seeking devious means to hide his real thoughts.

11. The movement of the plot was spoiled by too many sudden turns in the events.

12. We often admire modern works, but the works of earlier centuries tend to bore us.

13. The doors of the library are never opened before eight o'clock.

14. Despite his great army, Napoleon could not score a victory over the Russians.

15. Most authors in their autobiographical tales begin with the moment of their first love.